FINANCIAL PERFORMANCE ANALYSIS OF KANDLA PORT

:: Author ::

Hetal Shah
(M.com., NET.,M.Phil)

PUBLISHED BY

Hemchandracharya International Publishing House
HQ. At & Po. Chaveli., Ta- Chansma,
Dist- Patan, North Gujarat, India, Asia.
www.iphouseindia.com

First Publication: 5th July, 2015

ISBN:- 978-1-51486-608-5

Price: Rs.800/- INDIA

  $ 15 OUTSIDE INDIA

PUBLISHED BY

Hemchandracharya International Publishing House
HQ. At & Po. Chaveli., Ta- Chansma,
Dist- Patan, North Gujarat, India, Asia.
www.iphouseindia.com

INDEX

PREFACE

It is my great pleasure to present this book before our learned readers. A financial executive has to evaluate the performance, preset financial position, liquidity situation, and enquire into profitability of the firm and to plan for future operations. For all of this, they have to study the relationship among various financial variables in business as disclosed in various financial statements. To take the optimum financial decision, the financial analysis is essential for most of trading or non-trading organization whether they are in corporate form or non-corporate form. But they haven't proper guidance to do how the financial analysis in such way which helps them to provide best information of their financial reports to the end users. This book helps to serve this problem.

Keeping all this in view, the present book has been written with two clear objectives, viz., (i) to give exploratory study on Kandla Port Trust not only theoretical background on financial analysis; and (ii) to enable students, researchers, practitioners and end-users to use and synchronies not only accounting tools and techniques abut also statistical tools and techniques. It is hoped that the humble efforts made in the form of this book will assist in the accomplishment of financial analysis of corporate and non-corporate entities.

The book financial analysis – A study of Kandla Port Trust, is primarily the outcome of a research work carried out by us. A sincere attempt has been made to focus on the subject in six chapters, well arranged in a coherent manner.

Chapter one is an introduction, presenting an overview of the financial analysis. Chapter two presents conceptual understandings on financial analysis and brief explanations of the different accounting and statistical tools and techniques used in financial analysis. In chapter three, an effort has been made to present practically use of multiple correlation and multiple regression with the help of SPSS 17.0 software to do statistical analysis of incomes and expenses of Kandla Port Trust. These techniques are very difficult not only understand but also in use though we have been used it keenly and presented it in a very simple manner. This is very extraordinary specific part of our book and very rarely seen in other books in such way. Chapter four present theoretical background on ratio analysis and brief description of different ration on which they have been used in the study. In chapter five, an effort has been made to present practically use of different ratios on accounting data of Kandla Port Trust and also there are synchronizations of different statistical tools with ratio analysis. Chapter six present findings, suggestions and conclusion on different accounting and statistical tools and techniques have been used in the study.

I hope that the students, researchers, practitioners and end-users would find the reading of this book highly interesting and useful. The author feels that her efforts are amply rewarded if the book serves the purpose for which it is prepared. Suggestion for the improvement of the book from every corner is most appreciable.

HETAL SHAH

BHUJ-KACHCHH

LIST OF TABLES

LIST OF GRAPHS

CHAPTER – 01

INTRODUCTION

Accounting is the language of business. Language is one of the great tools of communication. Communication have main objective to give information to its' different users. In accountancy, financial statements proved one of the most useable means to give information to the different stakeholder of the firm.

If we assume accountancy as a tree, accounting principles and concepts are the root of the accounting tree and financial statements are the fruit of the accounting tree. In other words, accounting information is input and financial statements are output of it. Financial analysis is a sight by which end-users enable to analyse the financial statements and see the actual financial condition of the firm.

To take the optimum financial decision, the Financial Statements analyses are essential for most of trading or non-trading organisation whether they are in corporate form or non-corporate form. The external end-users of modern business enterprise are primarily interested in financial statements as aids to determine the financial condition and the results of operations of such business enterprises for specific periods of time, usually, one year. The internal end-users of financial statements are additionally interested in using the financial statements for effective organisational planning and control.

In order to achieve those objectives it is necessary to ensure that the end-users are able to analyse the financial data and statistics

1

contained in the financial statements for arriving at meaningful conclusion relating to various aspects of the operations of the company which in totality constitute the financial condition of enterprise. As, there has been long term development and huge growth in the port sector and it has shown remarkable contribution in the development of Indian economy – now a days it has become vital to do the financial evaluation of the port sector.

The coastline of India is dotted with 13 major ports and about 200 non-major ports. The capacity of major ports has increased from 20 million tons per annum (MTPA) in 1951 to 504.75 MTPA as on 31st March, 2007. At the beginning of the 10th Plan, the capacity of the major ports was 343.95 MTPA which has increased to 504.75 MTPA at the end of the 10th plan (i.e. as on 31st March, 2007) thereby achieving the capacity addition of 160.80 MTPA. In all the years of 10th five year plan the capacity at the major ports exceeded the traffic handled. The non-major ports handled traffic on 185.54 MTPA in 2006-07 and had a capacity of 228 MTPA at the end of 2006-07. (Source – India 2008)

For analysis purpose, keen study of financial analysis is necessary. To satisfy above purpose, the financial analysis of KANDLA PORT TRUST is selected.

CHAPTER – 2

FINANCIAL ANALYSIS: INTRODUCTION

2.1   CONCEPT OF FINANCIAL ANALYSIS:

The financial analysis is the process of identifying the financial strength and weakness of a firm from the available accounting data and financial statements. The focus of financial analysis is on key figures in the financial statements and the significant relationship that exists between them. The analysis of financial statements is a process of evaluating the relationship between component parts of financial statements to obtain a better understanding of the firm's position and performance. It is said that the process of the financial analysis is determining the significant operating and financial characteristic of a firm from accounting data.

The data of accounting is presented in the form of financial statements. There are two foremost financial statements i.e. Balance Sheet and Profit & Loss Account. The business concerns also prepare the Surplus Statement or Income Statement. The preparing financial accounts are the outcome for these statements.

The first task of the financial analyst is to determine the information relevant to the decision under consideration from the total information contained in the financial statements. The second step is to arrange information in a way to high light significant relationship. The final step is interpretation and drawing of inferences and conclusion.

Above all, the financial analysis is the process of selection, relation and evaluation. The financial position is revealed by them and profitability of the concern and utilization of retained earnings. However they are only the tools of communication, not the end of these financial statements by themselves. The analysis and interpretation of these various financial statements are concerned with the financial analysis. And thus, the past, present and projected performance of a business firm is devoted from the technique of a financial analysis evaluation. If we talk about the general usage in business, the term financial analysis is concerned with balance sheet, profit and loss account etc. But the meaning of the term is itself very vast and broad which is applied to almost any kind of detailed inquiry into financial data.

An executive of finance has to estimate the past performance, present financial position, liquidity situation, enquire into profitability of the firm and also to plan for future actions. Above these, the financial analysts have to study the relationship among the various financial variables in a business as disclosed in various financial statements.

2.2 DEFINITIONS OF FINANCIAL ANALYSIS:

According to John N. Myer " Financial Statement analysis is largely a study of relationships among the various financial factors in a business, as disclosed by a single set of statement and study of these factors as shown in a series of statements".

According to R.D. Kenedy and S.Y. Mcmuller, "The analysis and interpretation of financial statement are an attempt to determine the significance and meaning of the financial statement data so that the forecast may be made of the prospects for future earnings, ability to pay interest and debt maturities (both current and long-term) and profitability of a sound dividend policy".

According to Meigs, W.B. and others, "Financial analysis is the process of selection, relation and evaluation".

According to B. L. Mathur, "Financial analysis is the process of determining the significant operating and financial characteristics of a firm from accounting data."

According to The Institute of Chartered Accountants of India, "Financial analysis is the process of identifying the financial strength and weakness of a firm from the available accounting data and financial statements."

Thus, the focus of financial analysis is on key figures contained in financial statements and the significant relationship that exists between them. "Analyzing financial statement" to quote Metcalf and Titard, "is a process of evaluating relationship between component parts of financial statement to obtain a better understanding of a firm's position and performance".

2.3 STEPS OF FINANCIAL ANALYSIS:

A common process of financial analysis, to be done by any interested party, will be as follows –

1. Deciding upon the extent of analysis: First of all the depth, object and extent of analysis will be determined by the analyst. The determination of these basis facts determines the scope of analysis, tool of analysis and the amount and quality of financial data to be required. For example, to measure the financial position of the firm, the balance sheet of the firm will be analysed.

2. Going through the financial statement: Before analyzing and preparing any statement or composing financial ratios, it is necessary for the analyst to go through the various financial statements of the firm carefully.

3. Collection of necessary information: The analyst should collect other useful information from the management useful for analysis and interpretation but not being revealed from the published financial statements.

4. Rearrangement of financial data: Before making actual analysis and interpretation the analyst must rearrange the data provided by these statements in useful manner. The approximation of figures, re-classification or consolidation of items etc. is done in this step.

5. Analysis: Now the actual analysis is made. For analysis any of the technique of financial analysis can be used. It is depending upon requirement of analysis; it may be Statistical financial analysis techniques and Accounting financial analysis techniques. Ratio analysis is very important tool in this respect.

6. Interpretation and Presentation: After analyzing the interpretation is made and the inferences drawn from this analysis are presented in shape of reports of the management etc.

And also The Institute of Chartered Accountants of India gives steps to be taken for financial statement analysis are:

⇒ Identification of the user's purpose.

⇒ Identification of data source (which part of the Annual Report or other information is required to be analyzed to suit the purpose.)

⇒ Selecting the techniques to be used for such analysis.

2.4 TYPES OF FINANCIAL ANALYSIS:

Distinction between different types of financial analysis can be made either on the basis of material used for the analysis or according to *modus operandi* of the analysis or object of the analysis. It is important to distinguish between different types of the analysis because the techniques of analysis and interpretation differ according to the type of analysis. The following chart gives a snapshot view of financial analysis:

FINANCIAL ANALYSIS

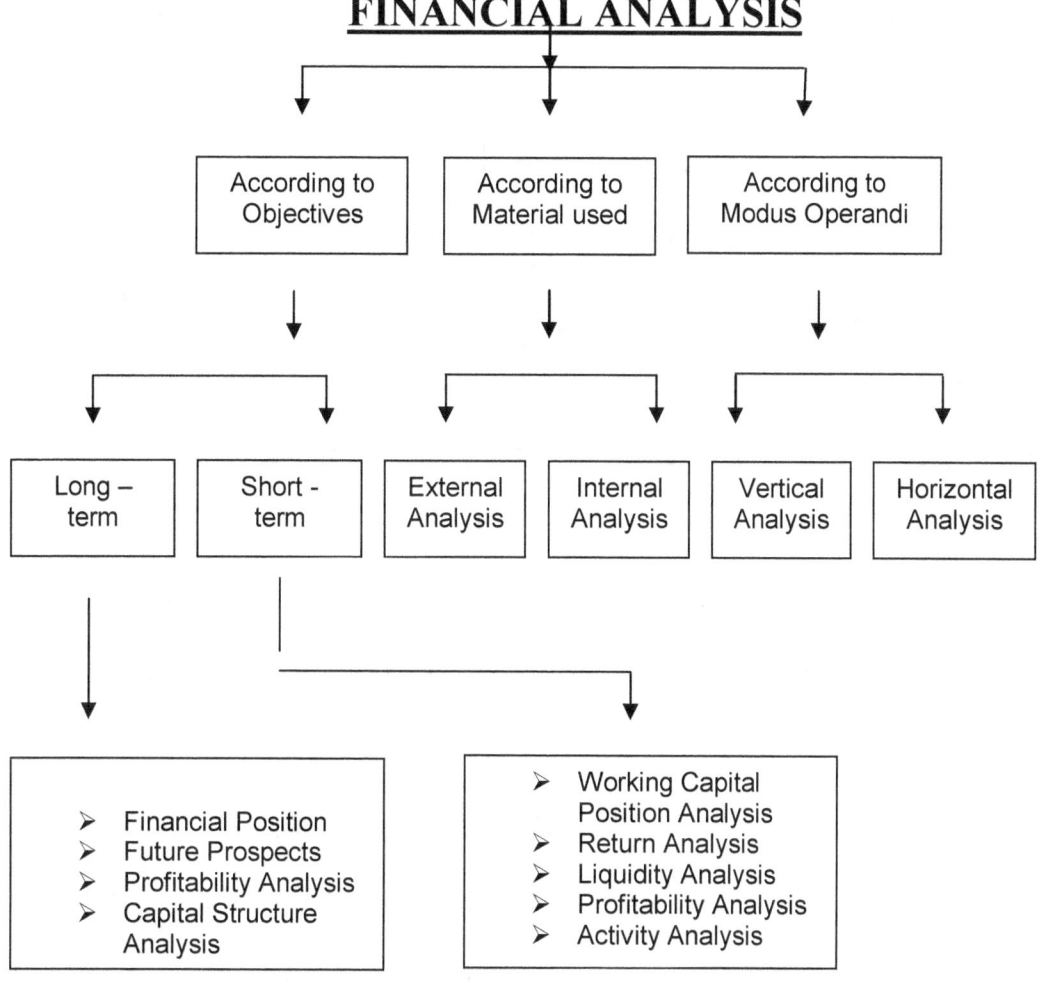

1. **External Analysis**: External analysis of financial statements is made by those who do not have access to the detailed accounting records of the company, i.e. banks, creditors and general public. These people depend almost entirely on published financial statements. The main objective of such analysis varies from party to party.

2. **Internal Analysis**: Such analysis is made by the finance and according department to help the top management. These people have direct approach to the relevant financial records so they can peep behind the two basic financial statement (B.S. & Income Statement) and narrate the inside story. Such analysis emphasizes

on the performance appraisal and assessing the profitability of different activities.

3. **Short-term Analysis**: The short-term analysis of financial statements is mainly concerned with the working capital analysis, activity analysis, return on investment analysis etc. In the short-run a company must have ample funds readily available to meet its current needs and sufficient borrowing capacity to meet the contingencies. Hence, in short-term analysis the current assets and current liabilities are analysed and cash position (liquidity) of the concern is determined. For short-term analysis the ratio analysis is very useful.

4. **Long-term Analysis**: In the long-run the company must earn a minimum amount sufficient to maintain a suitable rate of return on the investment, to provide for the necessary growth and development of the company and to meet the cost of capital. Financial planning is also necessary for the continued success of a company. Thus, in the long-run analysis the stress is on the stability and earning potentiality of the concern. In long-term analysis the fixed assets structure, leverage analysis, ownership pattern of securities etc. are analyzed.

The short-term and long-term, both types of analyses are important. Proper planning for future requires fairly sufficient knowledge of the company's current position which may be determined from short-term financial analysis only. The need of short-term analysis for long term planning is useful in the same way as a driver consulting a road map for the best route to his destination must know his present location too exactly.

5.   **Horizontal Analysis:** When financial statements for a number of years are reviewed and analyzed, the analysis is called 'horizontal analysis'. The preparation of Comparative Financial Statement and Trend Analysis are the examples of horizontal analysis. As it is based on data from year to year, rather than on one date or period of time as a whole, this is also known as 'dynamic analysis'. It is very useful for long-term planning as it involves the trend study of financial data.

6.   **Vertical Analysis:** It is also known as static analysis. When ratios are calculated from the balance sheet of one year (or profit and loss account of one year), it consists of vertical analysis. The preparation of Common Size Statement is an example of vertical analysis. It has got limited utility as it is concerned with short-term analysis only.

In this book for financial analysis we have chosen Kandla Post Trust as a case study. The study provide an idea about earning capacity, financial position, performance, liquidity, profitability, solvency and a comparative study within the research period form 1999-2000 to 2008-2009 of the Kandla Port Trust.

2.5   OBJECTIVE OF THE STUDY:

Overall objective of the study is to analyse the financial statements of KANDLA PORT TRUST within the research period.

The main objectives of this study are listed as under:

1. To measure the earning capacity of the firm.

2. To assess the financial position and performance of the firm.

3. To evaluate the liquidity, profitability and solvency of the firm.

4. To make a comparative study within the research period of the firm.

To get proper result hypotheses is one of the best ways. Because of that we are set up hypothesis on the basis of our objectives.

2.6 HYPOTHESIS OF THE STUDY:

1. Earning capacity of the firm is weak.

2. Financial position and performance of the firm are poor.

3. The liquidity, profitability and solvency of the firm are satisfactory.

4. Comparative study within the research period of the firm remains equal.

2.7 TOOLS AND TECHNIQUES OF FINANCIAL ANALYSIS:

There are many tools and techniques used for financial analysis but we are classified in to two different methods.

Following are the classified two different methods of financial analysis:

⇒ Accounting tools and techniques.

⇒ Statistical tools and techniques.

2.7.1 Accounting tools and techniques:

1. Comparative Financial and Operating Statements.

2. Common-size Statements.

3. Trend Ratios or Trend Analysis.

4. Average Analysis.

5. Statement of Changes in Working Capital.

6. Funds-flow and Cash –flow Analysis.

7. Ratio Analysis.

The brief description of above mentioned tools and techniques are as follows:

1. Comparative Financial and Operating Statements: The preparation of comparative financial and operating statements is an important device of horizontal financial analysis. Financial data become more meaningful when compared with similar data for a previous period or a number of prior periods. Statements prepared in a form that reflect financial data for two or more periods are known as Comparative Statements. Annual data can be compared with similar data for prior years. Such statements are very helpful in measuring the effects of the conduct of a business during the period under consideration. Comparative statements can be prepared for both types of financial statements –balance sheet as well as profit and loss accounts. The comparative profit and loss account will present a review of operating activities of the business. The comparative balance sheet shows the effect of operation on the assets and liabilities, i.e., change in the financial position during the period under consideration.

2. **Common Size Statements:** Comparative statements that give only the vertical percentage or ratios for financial data without giving rupee values are known as common size statements. They are also known as 100% statements. For example, if the balance sheet items are expressed as the ratio of each asset to total assets and the ratio of each liability to total liabilities (taking the total of balance sheet as100), it will be called a common size balance sheet. Thus, a common size statement shows the relation of each component to the whole. It is useful in vertical financial analysis and comparison of two business enterprises at a certain date.

3. **Trend Analysis:** Trend analysis is also an important tool of horizontal financial analysis. Under this technique of financial analysis, the ratios of different items for various periods are calculated and then a comparison is made. An analysis of the ratios over the past few years may well suggest the trend or direction in which the concern is going upward or downward.

4. **Average Analysis:** It is an improvement over trend analysis method. When trend ratios have been determined for the concern, these figures are compared with industry averages. These both trends can be presented on the graph paper also in the shape of curves. These presentations of facts in the shape of pictures make the analysis and comparison more comprehensive and impressive.

5. **Statement of Change in Working Capital:** To discuss the increase or decrease in working capital over a period of time, the preparation of a statement of changes in working capital is also very useful. The main objective of this statement preparation is to derive a fairly accurate summary of the events that affected the amount of working capital. The amount of net working capital is determined by deducting the total of current liabilities from the total of the current assets. Hence, it is a rough statement which may be prepared by using balance sheet data only. But it does not explain the detailed reasons for the changes in working capital and method of financing additional requirements of working capital. Hence, the preparation of funds-flow statement becomes necessary.

6. **Fund-flow and Cash-flow Analysis:** Funds-flow analysis is a valuable and to the financial executive and creditors for evaluating the uses of funds by the firm and in determining how these use were financed. A funds-flow statement indicates where funds came from and where it was used during the period under review. Cash flow statement is a statement which indicates sources of cash inflow and transactions of cash outflows of a firm during an accounting period. These statements can be prepared separately also. They are important tools of communication and very helpful for financial executives planning the intermediate and long-term financing of the firm.

7. **Ratio analysis:** Ratio analysis is an important and widely used tools of analysis of financial statements. It is essentially an attempt

to develop meaningful relationship between individual items (or groups of items) in the balance sheet of profit and loss account. The objects and utility of ratio analysis as a technique of financial analysis is confined not only to the internal parties but to the credit suppliers, banks and lending institutions also. If functions as a sort of the health test. In the nut-shell ratio analysis gibes the answers of the following problems: whether the enterprise's financial position is sound, whether the capital structure of the business is in proper order, whether the profitability of the enterprises is satisfactory, whether the credit policy in relation to sales and purchases is sound and whether the company is creditworthy. Thus, ratio analysis highlights the liquidity, solvency, profitability and capital gearing position.

2.7.2 Statistical tools and techniques:

⇒ Mean

⇒ Standard deviation

⇒ Coefficient of Variation (C.V.)

⇒ Coefficient of Correlation (r)

⇒ Coefficient of Determination (r^2)

⇒ Adjusted Coefficient of Determination (adjusted R^2)

⇒ Multiple Correlation

⇒ Multiple Regression

⇒ Analysis of Variance (ANOVA)

The brief description of above mentioned tools and techniques are as follows:

MEAN:

The arithmetic mean is a measure of central tendency and is popularly known as mean. Arithmetic mean is obtained by dividing the sum of the values of all items of a series by the number of items of that series. It is can be computed for unclassified or ungrouped data or individual series as well as classified or grouped data or discrete or continuous series.

STANDARD DEVIATION:

The numerical value of population or a sample variance is difficult to interpret because it is expressed in square units. To reach an interpretable measure of variance expressed in the units of original data, we take a positive square root of the variance, which is known as the standard deviation or root-mean square deviation. We can think of the standard deviation as roughly the average values of fall from the mean.

COEFFICIENT OF VARIATION (CV):

Standard deviation is an absolute measure of variation and expresses variation in the same unit of measurement as the arithmetic mean or the original data. A relative measure called the coefficient of variation (CV). Coefficient of variation (CV) measures the standard deviation relative to the mean in percentages. In other words, CV indicates how large the standard deviation is in relation to the mean.

Coefficient of variation (CV) is developed by Karl Pearson is very useful measure for (i) comparing data sets that are in same unit of measurement but the mean values of data sets in comparable filed are widely dissimilar (ii) comparing two or more data sets expressed in different units of measurement.

COEFFICIENT OF CORRELATION (r):

Correlation is the relationship that exists between two or more variables. If two variables are related to each other in such a way that change in one creates a corresponding change in the other, then the variables are said to be correlated.

Interpretation of coefficient of correlation(r):

The value of r lies between - 1 to + 1.

VALUE OF r	INTERPRETAION
(a) If $r = +1$	There exists **perfect positive correlation** between the variable.
(b) If $r = -1$	There exists **perfect negative correlation** between the variable.
(c) If $r = 0$	There exists **no correlation** between the variable.
(d) If $+0.75 \leq r < +1$	There exists **high positive correlation** between the variable.
(e) If $-0.75 \geq r < -1$	
(f) If $+0.50 \leq r < +0.75$	

(g) If $-0.50 \geq r < -0.75$	There exists **high negative correlation** between the variable.
(h) If $r < +0.50$	There exists **moderate positive correlation** between the variable.
(i) If $r > -0.50$	There exists **moderate negative correlation** between the variable.
	There exists **low positive correlation** between the variable.
	There exists **low negative correlation** between the variable.

COEFFICIENT OF DETERMINATION (r^2):

The squared value of the correlation coefficient r is called coefficient of determination, denoted as r^2. This measure represent the proportion (or percentage) of the total variability of the dependent variable, y that is accounted for or explained by the independent variable, x. The proportion (percentage) of variation in y that x can explain determines more precisely the extent or strength of association between two variables x and y. It is also defined as the ratio of the explained variance to the total variance. It always has value between 0 and 1.

Interpretation of Coefficient of Determination:

Coefficient of determination is preferred for interpreting the strength of association between two variables because it is easier to interpret a percentage.

⇒ If r^2 = 0, then no variation in y can be explain by the variable x. There is no association between x and y.

⇒ If r^2 = 1, then values of y are completely explained by x. There is perfect association between x and y.

⇒ If $0 \leq r^2 \leq 1$, the degree of explained variation in y as a result of variation in values of x depends on the value of r^2. Value of r^2 closer to 0 shows low proportion of variation in y explained by x. On the other hand value of r^2 closer to 1 show that variable x can predict the actual value of the variable y.

Adjusted Coefficient of Determination (adjusted R^2)

Modified measure of the coefficient of determination that takes into account the number of independent variables included in the regression equation and the sample size. Although the addition of independent variables will always causes the coefficient of determination to rise, the adjusted coefficient of determination may fall if the added independent variables have little explanatory power and/or if the degrees of freedom become too small. This statistic is quite useful for comparison between equations with different numbers of independent variables, differing sample sizes, or booth.

MULTIPLE CORRELATION:

When three or more variables are studied, it is case of multiple correlation. Through multiple correlation analysis we can attempt to measure the degree of association between a dependent (response) variable y and two or more independent variables (predictors) X_1, X_2, X_3, ...,X_k, taken together as a group. For example, when one studies relationship between the yield of wheat per acre, amount of rainfall and amount of fertilizers used, it is a problem of multiple correlation. Multiple correlation may be either partial or total.

1. Partial Multiple Correlation:

In case of partial multiple correlation one studies three or more variables but considers only two variables to influencing each other and the effect of other influencing variables being held constant. Its order depends on the number of variables which are held constant e.g. if one variable is kept constant, it is called first order partial correlation.

2. Total Multiple Correlation:

In case of total multiple correlation one studies three or more variables without excluding the effect of any variables held as constant.

MULTIPLE REGRESSION:

Multiple regression analysis is a statistical technique that can be used to analyze the relationship between a single dependent (criterion) variable and several independent (predictor) variables. Multiple regression is the appropriate method of analysis when the research problem involves a single metric dependent variable presumed to be related to two or more metric independent variable.

The objective of multiple regression analysis is to predict the changes in the dependent variable in response to changes in the independent variables. In other words, the objective of multiple regression analysis is to use the independent variables whose values are known to predict the single dependent values selected by the researcher. This objective is most often achieved through statistical rule of least squares.

Each independent variable is weighed by the regression analysis procedure to ensure maximum prediction from the set of independent variables. The weights denote the relative contribution of the independent variables to the overall prediction and facilitate interpretation as to the influence of each variable in making the prediction, although correlation among the independent variables complicates the interpretative process. The set of weighted independent variables forms the regression variant, a linear combination of the independent variables that best predicts the dependent variables. The regression variant also referred to as the regression equation or regression model, is the most widely known example of a variant among the multivariate techniques.

Whenever the researcher is interested in prediction the amount or magnitude of the dependent variable, multiple regression is useful. For example, sales turnover of a product (dependent variables) is associated with multiple independent variables such as price of product, expenditure on advertisement, quality of the product, competitors and so on.

Analysis of Variance (ANOVA):

Professor R.A. Fisher was the first man to use term 'variance' and, in fact, it was he who developed a very elaborate theory concerning ANOVA or F-test, explaining its usefulness in practical field. Later on Professor Snedecor and many others contributed to the development of this technique. ANOVA is test for the significance of the difference among more than two sample means and to make inferences about whether such samples are from the populations having the same mean. F–test is based on the ratio rather than the difference between variances.

ANOVA is essentially a procedure for testing the difference among different groups of data for homogeneity. The essence of ANOVA is that the total amount of variation in a set of data is broken down into two types, that amount which can be attributed to chance and that amount which can be attributed to specified causes. Hence, it is a method of analyzing the variance to which a response is subject into its various components corresponding to various sources of variation.

CHAPTER – 3
STATISTICAL ANALYSIS OF INCOMES – EXPENSES

3.1 INTRODUCTION:

In the scientific, social and economic phenomena do not confine to two variables only. A large number of studies involve more than two variables. In these studies, we often need to give actual relationship between two or more variables and/or to explain the strength of association between them. For this, multivariate correlation and regression are strong tools. For instance, the cost of production of a manufactured product mainly depends on the cost of raw material, the labour charges and the cost of energy. The cost of a crop mainly depends upon the cost of seeds, fertilizer, irrigation, pesticides and many farm operations. In both the examples, the cost of the produced product is a dependent factor, while others are independent factors.

Multiple Correlation in Terms of Simple Correlation:

If we consider only k variables X_1, X_2, X_3, ...,X_k, the simple correlation coefficients between all possible pairs of k-variables can easily be arranged in a correlation matrix P as given below.

		1	r_{12}	r_{13}	...	r_{1k}
		r_{21}	1	r_{23}	...	r_{2K}
		r_{31}	r_{32}	1	...	r_{3K}
	P =	.				
		.				
		.				
		r_{12}	r_{12}	r_{12}	...	1

Recall r_{ij} and $r_{ii} = r_{jj} = 1$ for $i,j = 1,2,3,\ldots,k$. Therefore, P is always a symmetric square matrix.

3.2 STATISTICAL ANALYSIS OF TOTAL INCOME OF KPT:

Table 3.2.1 Correlation Matrix of Total Income

	Total Income	Cargo handling & storage charges	Port & dock charges	Estate rental	Financial & miscellaneous income
Total Income	1.000	.956	.988	.426	.516
Cargo handling & storage charges	.956	1.000	.937	.395	.299
Port & dock charges	.988	.937	1.000	.513	.446
Estate rental	.426	.395	.513	1.000	-.190
Financial & miscellaneous income	.516	.299	.446	-.190	1.000

Total income of the KPT consist of five main incomes which are Cargo handling & storage charges, Port & dock charges, Estate rental, Township and Financial & miscellaneous income. For calculation of correlation matrix of total income of the KPT, researcher has taken all main income except Township. Township incomes were earned only three initial years during the research period, so that it was excluded for the calculation of correlation matrix of total income of the KPT.

The correlation matrix reveals the uni-directional relationship among the various sources of total income of the KPT during the research period that is 1999-2000 to 2008-2009. On the table 3.2.1 it may be observed that except correlation co-efficient of Estate rental and Financial & miscellaneous incomes, all the correlation co-efficient have positive sign.

Correlation co-efficient between Cargo handling & storage charges and Total income is as high as 0.956 and also between Port & dock charges and Total income is as high as 0.988. While other hand of matrix, correlation co-efficient between Estate rental and Total income is as low as 0.426 and also between Financial & miscellaneous incomes and Total income is as low as 0.516 comparatively to above mentioned two correlations co-efficient of this column.

Second column of correlation matrix has shown the correlations co-efficient between Cargo handling & storage charges and other main income of the KPT. Correlation co-efficient between Port & dock charges and Cargo handling & storage charges is as high as 0.937. Correlation co-efficient between Estate rental and Cargo handling & storage charges is as low as 0.395 and also between Financial & miscellaneous incomes and Cargo handling & storage charges is as low as 0.299 comparatively to correlations co-efficient between Port & dock charges and Cargo handling & storage charges.

Third column of correlation matrix has shown the correlations co-efficient between Port & dock charges and other main income of the KPT. Correlation co-efficient between Estate rental and Port & dock charges is 0.513. Correlation co-efficient between Financial & miscellaneous incomes and Port & dock charges is 0.446.

Fourth column of correlation matrix has shown the correlations co-efficient between Estate rental and other main income of the KPT. In this column it can be seen that correlation co-efficient between Estate rental and Financial & miscellaneous incomes is -0.190 which was shown low negative correlation.

Last column of correlation matrix is Financial & miscellaneous incomes. Correlation co-efficient shown in this column have been also come in earlier stated column so that they have not been described here again.

Simple correlation has shown only uni-directional relationship between two variables but it is not revealed multiple relationships among three or more variables. In this situation multiple correlations help us to measure multiple relationships among three or more variables. So that researcher has worked out multiple correlation coefficient - R to measure the multiple relationships among total income and four main incomes (which are shown in table 3.2.1) of KPT. Calculations of multiple correlation coefficient - R have been done with the help of SPSS Statistics 17.0 version software below:

Multiple R	1
R Square	1
Adjusted R Square	1
Std. error of Estimate	106.32266

The values of multiple R, R square and adjusted R square are one. These indicates that there exists a perfect positive correlation and linear association between Total income (dependent variable) and Cargo handling & storage charges, Port & dock charges, Estate rental, and Financial & miscellaneous income (independent variables). Because of that we can also use linear regression model.

Correlation shows the degree and direction of relationship between the variables but cannot show the nature and extent of functional relationship between two or more variables and cannot able to predict the values of a dependent variable from the given value of an independent variable. In such a situation, regression methods serve our purpose.

For that researcher has also calculated multiple regressions among the Total income and four main incomes (which were earlier stated) of KPT. Calculations of multiple regressions have been done with the help of SPSS Statistics 17.0 version software, are as follows:

$$Y = \beta_0 + \beta_1 X_1 + \beta_2 X_2 + \beta_3 X_3 + \beta_4 X_4$$

Whereas,

Y = Total income (dependent variable)

X_1 = Cargo handling & storage charges (independent variable)

X_2 = Port & dock charges (independent variable)

X_3 = Estate rental (independent variable)

X_4 = Financial & miscellaneous income (independent variable)

β_0 = Y Intercept

β_1 = slope of Y with variable X_1 holding variables X_2, X_3, X_4

β_2 = slope of Y with variable X_2 holding variables X_1, X_3, X_4

β_3 = slope of Y with variable X_3 holding variables X_1, X_2, X_4

β_4 = slope of Y with variable X_4 holding variables X_1, X_2, X_3

$$Y = \beta_0 + \beta_1 X_1 + \beta_2 X_2 + \beta_3 X_3 + \beta_4 X_4$$

$$\therefore Y = 1299.162 + 0.948\, X_1 + 1.081\, X_2 + 0.744\, X_3 + 0.931\, X_4$$

... (3.1)

(With the help of SPSS Statistics 17.0 version software)

Using equation (3.1), we can able to predict the value of Total income (Y, dependent variable) from the given values of the Cargo handling & storage charges (X_1, independent variable), Port & dock charges (X_2, independent variable), Estate rental (X_3, independent variable), Financial & miscellaneous income (X_4, independent variable).

Now that we have used ANOVA to assure ourselves that the multiple linear regression model is appropriate, we can determine whether there is a significant relationship between the dependent variable and the set of independent variable. The null and alternative hypotheses can be set up as follows:

$H_0 : \beta_1 = \beta_2 = \beta_3 = \beta_4 = 0$ (There is no linear relationship between the dependent variable and the independent variables)

H_1 : At least one $\beta_j \neq 0$ (There is a linear relationship between the dependent variable and the independent variables)

Table 3.2.2 ANOVA for Multiple Regression of Total Income

Source of Variation	Sum of Squares (SS)	d.f.	Mean Square (MS)	F
Regression	595812320.365371	4	148953080.091343	13176.432
Residual	56522.538	5	11304.508	
Total	595868842.903	9		

If a level of significance of 0.05 is chosen, we can determine from table 3.2.2 that the critical value on the F distribution (with 4 and 5 degrees of freedom) is 13176.432. Whereas, table value of F for (4, 5) d.f. and $\alpha = 0.05$ is 5.19. Since the calculated value of F is greater than tabulated of F, $F_C > F_t$. The difference between the calculated value of F and tabulated value of F is significant so that H_0 is rejected and H_1 is accepted.

It means that one or more β's are significant and at least one of the independent variables related to dependent variable. In simple words, Cargo handling & storage charges, Port & dock charges, Estate rental and Financial & miscellaneous income, among these four main sources of incomes at least one of the incomes is related to Total income.

3.3 STATISTICAL ANALYSIS OF TOTAL EXPENSES OF KPT:

Table 3.3.1 Correlation Matrix of Total Expenses

	Total Expenses	Cargo Handling & Storage Charges	Port & Dock Facilities for Shipping	Railway Working	Rentable Land & Building	Management & Gen. Adm. Exp.	Finance & Misc. Exe
Total Expenses	1.000	.803	.884	.149	.859	.864	.358
Cargo Handling & Storage Charges	.803	1.000	.930	.218	.941	.910	-.236
Port & Dock Facilities for Shipping	.884	.930	1.000	.218	.958	.901	-.090
Railway Working	.149	.218	.218	1.000	.233	.304	-.173
Rentable Land & Building	.859	.941	.958	.233	1.000	.965	-.134
Management & Gen. Adm. Exp.	.864	.910	.901	.304	.965	1.000	-.057
Finance & Misc. Exe	.358	-.236	-.090	-.173	-.134	-.057	1.000

Total expenses of the KPT consist of seven main expenses which are Cargo handling & storage charges, Port & dock facilities for shipping, Railway working, Rentable land & building, Township, Management & general administrative expenses and Finance & miscellaneous expenses. For calculation of correlation matrix of total expenses of the KPT, researcher has taken all main expenses except Township. Township expenses were incurred only three initial years during the research period, so that it was excluded for the calculation of correlation matrix of total expenses of the KPT.

The correlation matrix reveals the uni-directional relationship among the various types of total expenses of the KPT during the research period that is 1999-2000 to 2008-2009. On the table 3.3.1 it is seen that the first column of correlation matrix is Total expenses. This column has shown the correlation co-efficient between total expenses and other main expenses of the KPT. Correlation co-efficient between Total expenses and Cargo handling & storage charges, Total expenses and Port & dock facilities for shipping, Total expenses and Railway working, Total expenses and Rentable land & building, Total expenses and Management & general administrative expenses and also Total expenses and Finance & miscellaneous expenses are 0.083, 0.884, 0.149, 0.859, 864, and 0.0358 respectively.

Second column of correlation matrix has shown the correlations co-efficient between Cargo handling & storage charges and other main expenses of the KPT. Correlation co-efficient between Cargo handling & storage charges and Port & dock facilities for shipping,

Cargo handling & storage charges and Railway working, Cargo handling & storage charges and Rentable land & building, Cargo handling & storage charges and Management & general administrative expenses and also Cargo handling & storage charges and Finance & miscellaneous expenses are 0.930, 0.218, 0.941, 0.910 and -0.236 respectively.

Third column of correlation matrix has shown the correlations co-efficient between Port & dock facilities for shipping and other main expenses of the KPT. Correlation co-efficient between Port & dock facilities for shipping and Railway working, Port & dock facilities for shipping and Rentable land & building, Port & dock facilities for shipping and Management & general administrative expenses and also Port & dock facilities for shipping and Finance & miscellaneous expenses are 0.218, 0.958, 0.901 and -0.090 respectively.

Forth column of correlation matrix has shown the correlations co-efficient between Railway working and other main expenses of the KPT. Correlationco-efficient between Railway working and Rentable land & Building, Railway working and Management & general administrative expenses and also Railway working and Finance & miscellaneous expenses are 0.233, 0.304 and -0.173 respectively.

Fifth column of correlation matrix has shown the correlations co-efficient between Rentable land & building and other main expenses of the KPT. Correlationco-efficient between Rentable land & building and Management & general administrative expenses is

0.965. Correlationco-efficient between Rentable land & building and Finance & miscellaneous expenses is -0.134.

Sixth column of correlation matrix has shown the correlations co-efficient between Management & general administrative expenses and other main expenses of the KPT. Correlationco-efficient between Management & general administrative and finance & miscellaneous expenses is -0.057.

Last column of correlation matrix is Financial & miscellaneous expenses. Correlation co-efficient shown in this column have been also come in earlier stated column so that they have not been described here again.

Simple correlation has shown only uni-directional relationship between two variables but it is not revealed multiple relationships among three or more variables. In this situation multiple correlation help us to measure multiple relationships among three or more variables. So that researcher has worked out multiple correlation coefficient - R to measure the multiple relationships among total expenses and six main expenses (which are shown in table 3.3.1) of KPT. Calculations of multiple correlation coefficient - R have been done with the help of SPSS Statistics 17.0 version software, are as follows:

Multiple R	1
R Square	1
Adjusted R Square	1
Std. error of Estimate	87.31286

The values of multiple R, R square and adjusted R square are one. These indicates that there exists a perfect positive correlation and linear association between Total expenses (dependent variable) and Cargo handling & storage charges, Port & dock facilities for shipping, Railway working, Rentable land & building, Management & general administrative expenses and Finance & miscellaneous expenses (independent variables). Because of that we can also use linear regression model.

Correlation show the degree and direction of relationship between the variables but can not show the nature and extent of functional relationship between two or more variables and can not able to predict the values of a dependent variable from the given value of an independent variable. In such a situation, regression methods serve our purpose.

For that researcher has also calculated multiple regressions among the total expenses and six main expenses (which were earlier stated) of KPT. Calculations of multiple regressions have been done with the help of SPSS Statistics 17.0 version software, are as follows:

$$Y = \beta_0 + \beta_1 X_1 + \beta_2 X_2 + \beta_3 X_3 + \beta_4 X_4 + \beta_5 X_5 + \beta_6 X_6$$

Whereas,

Y = Total expenses (dependent variable)

X_1 = Cargo handling & storage charges (independent variable)

X_2= Port& dock facilities for shipping (independent variable)

X_3 = Railway working (independent variable)

X_4 = Rentable land & building (independent variable)

X_5 = Management & general administrative expenses (independent variable)

X_6 = Finance & miscellaneous expenses (independent variable)

β_0 = Y Intercept

β_1 = slope of Y with variable X_1 holding variables X_2, X_3, X_4, X_5, X_6

β_2 = slope of Y with variable X_2 holding variables X_1, X_3, X_4, X_5, X_6

β_3 = slope of Y with variable X_3 holding variables X_1, X_2, X_4, X_5, X_6

β_4 = slope of Y with variable X_4 holding variables X_1, X_2, X_3, X_5, X_6

β_5 = slope of Y with variable X_5 holding variables X_1, X_2, X_3, X_4, X_6

β_6 = slope of Y with variable X_6 holding variables X_1, X_2, X_3, X_4, X_5

$$Y = \beta_0 + \beta_1 X_1 + \beta_2 X_2 + \beta_3 X_3 + \beta_4 X_4 + \beta_5 X_5 + \beta_6 X_6$$

$$\therefore\ Y = 647.972 + 1.071X_1 + 0.951X_2 + 1.042X_3 + 1.321X_4 + 0.772X_5 + 1.005X_6$$

(Equation No. 3.2)

Using equation (3.2), we can able to predict the value of Total expenses (Y, dependent variable) from the given values of the Cargo handling & storage charges (X_1, independent variable), Port & dock facilities for shipping (X_2, independent variable), Railway working (X_3, independent variable), Rentable land & building (X_4, independent variable), Management & general administrative expenses (X_5, independent variable) and Finance & miscellaneous expenses (X_6, independent variable).

Now that we have used ANOVA to assure ourselves that the multiple linear regression model is appropriate, we can determine whether there is a significant relationship between the dependent variable and the set of independent variable. The null and alternative hypotheses can be set up as follows:

$H_0 : \beta_1 = \beta_2 = \beta_3 = \beta_4 = \beta_5 = \beta_6 = 0$ (There is no linear relationship between the dependent variable and the independent variables)

H_1 : At least one $\beta_j \neq 0$ (There is a linear relationship between the dependent variable and the independent variables)

Table 3.3.2 ANOVA for Multiple Regression of Total Expenses

Source of Variation	Sum of Squares (SS)	d.f.	Mean Square (MS)	F
Regression	455946018.473068	6	75991003.0788447	9967.948
Residual	22870.606	3	7623.535	
Total	455968889.07889	9		

If a level of significance of 0.05 is chosen, we can determine from table 3.3.2 that the critical value on the F distribution (with 6 and 3 degrees of freedom) is 9967.948. Whereas, table value of F for (6, 3) d.f. and $\alpha = 0.05$ is 8.94. Since the calculated value of F is greater than tabulated of F, $F_C > F_t$. The difference between the calculated value of F and tabulated value of F is significant so that H_0 is rejected and H_1 is accepted.

It means that one or more β's are significant and at least one of the independent variables related to dependent variable. In simple words, Cargo handling & storage charges, Port & dock facilities for shipping, Railway working, Rentable land & building, Management & general administrative expenses and Finance & miscellaneous expenses among these six main expenses at least one of the expense is related to Total expenses.

CHAPTER – 4
THEORIES OF RATIO ANALYSIS

4.1 INTRODUCTION:

The company's financial information is contained in Balance Sheet and Profit and Loss Account. The figures contained in these statements are absolute and sometimes unconnected with one another. An absolute figure does not convey much meaning. However, it is only in the light of other information that the significance of a figure is realized. For instance, Mr. X weighs 50kg. Is he fat? We cannot give answer unless we know his age and height. Similarly a company's profitability cannot be known unless together with the amount or profit, the capital employed is also seen.

The relationship of these two figures expressed mathematically is known as RATIO. The ratio refers to the numerical or quantitative relationship between two variables or items. A ratio is calculated by dividing one item of the relationship with other. The ratio analysis is one of the most useful and common method of analyzing financial statements.

As compared to other tools of financial analysis, the ratio analysis provides very useful conclusions about various aspects of the working of an enterprise. The need for ratio arises due to the fact that absolute figures are often misleading. Absolute figures are certainly valuable but their value increases manifold if they are studied with another through ration analysis.

Ratios enable the mass of data to be summarized and simplified. Ratio analysis is an instrument for diagnosis of the financial health of an enterprise. Ratios, in fact, are full of meaning and communicate the relative importance of the various items appearing in the Balance Sheet and Profit and Loss Account.

4.2 MEANING OF RATIO:

Ratio analysis is a widely-used tool of financial analysis. It can be used to compare the risk and return relationships of firms of different sizes. It is defined as the systematic use of ratio to interpret the financial statements so that the strengths and weakness of a firm as well as its historical performance and current financial condition can be determined.

A ratio is only a comparison of the numerator with the denominator. The term ratio refers to the numerical or quantitative relationship between two figures. A ratio is the relationship between two figures, and obtained by dividing the former by the latter. Ratios are designed to show how one number is related to another. It is worked out by dividing one number by another.

Ratio analysis is an important and age old technique of financial analysis. The data given in financial statements, in absolute form, are dump and are unable to communicate anything. Ratios are relative form of financial data and very useful technique to check upon the efficiency of a firm. Some ratios indicate the trend or progress or downfall of the firm.

4.3 MODE OF EXPRESSION:

(1)   Rate, which is the ratio between the two numerical facts over a period of time, for example, stock turnover is there times a year.

(2)   PURE RATIOS OR PROPORTION which is arrived at by the simple division of one number by another, for example, Current Asset to Current Liability ratios is 3 : 1.

(3)   PERCENTAGE which is a special type of rate expressing the relationship in hundred. It is arrived at by multiplying the quotient by 100, for example, gross profit is 30 % of sales.

These alternative methods of expressing items which are related to each other are, for purposes of financial analysis, referred to as ratio analysis. In other words, ratios, as a tool of financial management, cab be expressed as 1) Pure Ratio 2) Percentage and 3) a stated comparison between numbers. Each method of expression has a distinct advantage over the other. The analyst will elect that mode which will best suit his purpose and convenience.

It should be noted that computing ratios do not add any information not already inherent in the figures. What the ratios do is that they reveal the relationship in a more meaningful way so as to enable us to draw conclusions from them. A single figure by itself has no meaning but when expressed in terms of a related figure it yields significant inferences. For instance, a firm earns Rs.3,00,000 as net profit. This fact throws no light on its adequacy or otherwise. The figure of net profit has to be considered in relation to sales or capital employed or other variables. Then a meaningful conclusion cab be drawn by converting the figures into meaningful comparable forms and removes the difficulty of drawing inferences on the basis of absolute figures

4.4 STEPS IN RATIO ANALYSIS:

The first task of the financial analyst is to select the information relevant to the decision under consideration form the statements and calculates appropriate ratios.

The second step is to compare the calculated ratios with the ratios of the same firm relating to past or with the industry ratios. This step facilitates in assessing success or failure of the firm.

The third step involves interpretation, drawing of inferences and report-writing. Conclusions are drawn after comparison in the shape of report or recommended course of action.

4.5 IMPORTANCE OF RATIO ANALYSIS:

The inter relationship that exists among the different items appeared in the financial statements, are revealed by accounting ratios. Ratio analysis of a firm's financial statements is of interest to a number of parties, mainly, shareholders, creditors, financial executives etc. Shareholders are interested with earning capacity of the firm: creditors are interested in knowing the ability of firm to meet its financial obligations; and financial executives are concerned with evolving analytical tools that will measure and compare costs, efficiently, liquidity and profitability with a view to making intelligent decisions.

The importances of ratio analysis are discussed below, in brief:

1) **Aid to measure General Efficiency**: Ratios enable the mass accounting data to be summarized and simplified. They act as an index of the efficiency of the enterprise. As such they serve as an instrument of management control.

2) **Aid to measure Financial Solvency** : Ratios are useful tools in the hands of management and other concerned to evaluate the firms performance over a period of time by comparing the present ratio with the past ones. They point out firm's liquidity position to meet its short-term obligations and long-term solvency.

3) **Aid in Forecasting and Planning**: Ration analysis is an invaluable aid to management in the discharge of its basic function such as planning, forecasting, control etc. The ratios that are derived after analyzing and scrutinizing the past result, helps the management to prepare budgets to formulate policies and to prepare the future plant of action etc.

4) **Facilitate decision-making:** It throws light on the degree of efficiency of the management and utilization of the assets and that is why it is called surveyor of efficiency. They help management in decision-making.

5) **Aid in Corrective Action**: Ratio analysis provides interfirm comparison. They highlight the factors associated with successful and unsuccessful firms. If comparison shows an

unfavorable variance, corrective actions can be initiated. Thus, it helps the management to take corrective action.

6) **Aid in Intra Firm Comparison:** Intra firm comparisons are facilitated. It is an instrument for diagnosis of financial health of an enterprise. It facilitates the management to know whether the firm's financial position is improving or deteriorating by setting a trend with the help of ratios.

7) **Act as a Good Communication:** Ratios are an effective means of communication and play a vital role in informing the position of and progress made by the business concern to the owners and other interested parties. The communications by the use of simplified and summarized ratios are more easy and understandable.

8) **Evaluation of Efficiency:** Ratio analysis is an effective instrument which, when properly used, is useful to assess important characteristics of business – liquidity, solvency, profitability etc. A study of these aspects may enable conclusions to be drawn relating to capabilities of business.

9) **Effective Tool:** Ratio analysis helps in making effective control of the business – measuring performance, control of cost etc. Effective control is the keynote of better management. Ratio ensures secrecy.

Figures, in their absolute forms, shown in the financial statements are neither significant nor able to compared. In fact, they are dump. But ratios have power to speak.

4.6 NATURE OF RATIO ANALYSIS:

Ratio analysis is a powerful tool of financial analysis. A Ratio is defined as "the indicated quotient to two mathematical expressions" and as "relationship between two or more things". In financial analysis, a ratio is used as an index or yardstick for evaluating the financial position and performance of a firm. Analysis of financial statements is a process of evaluating relationship between component parts of financial statements to obtain a better understating of the firm's position and performance. Financial analysis is used as a device to analyze and interpret the financial health of enterprise.

The absolute accounting figures reported in the financial statements do not provided a meaningful understating of the performance and financial performance of a firm. An accounting figure conveys meaning when it is related to some other relevant information. Just like a doctor examines his patient by recording his body temperature, blood pressure etc., before making his conclusion regarding the illness and before giving his treatment, a financial analyst analyses the financial statements with various tools of analysis before commenting upon the financial health or weaknesses of an enterprise. A ratio is known as a symptom like blood pressure, the pulse rate or the temperature of an individual. It is with help of ratios that the financial statements can be analyzed more clearly and decisions are drawn from such analysis. The point to note is that a ratio indicates a quantitative relationship, which can be in turn used to make a qualitative judgment. Such is the nature of all financial ratios.

4.7 LIMITATIONS OF RATION ANALYSIS:

Ratio analysis is, as already mentioned, a widely – used tool of financial analysis. It is because ratios are simple and easy to understand. But they must be used very carefully. They suffer from various limitations. For instance, financial statements suffer from a number of limitations and may therefore, affect the quality of ratio analysis. If due care is not taken, they might confuse rather than clarify the situation. Different firms may use these terms in different senses or the same firm may use them to mean different things at different times. Some of the limitations of the ratio analysis are given below:

1) **Differences in Definitions:** Comparisons are made difficult due to differences in definitions of various financial terms. Lack of standard formula for working out ratios makes it difficult to compare them. They are worked out on the basis of different items in different industries.

2) **Limitations of Accounting Records:** Ratio analysis is based on financial statements which are themselves subject to limitations. Thus, ratios calculated on the figures given in the financial statements, also suffers from similar limitations.

3) **Lack of Proper Standards:** It is very difficult to ascertain the standard ratio in order to make proper comparison. Because, it differs from firm to firm, industry to industry. Apart from this, it may also have happened that in one firm, a current ratio of 2 : 1 is found to be quite satisfactory, whereas in another firm 2.5 : 1

may be unsatisfactory. Again, a high current ratio may not necessarily mean sound liquid position when current assets include large inventory or inventory consisting of obsolete items.

4) **No Allowances for Price Level Changes:** Due to changes in price level of various years, comparison of ratios of such years cannot give correct conclusions. A change in the price level can seriously affect the validity of comparison of ratios computed for different the periods. For instance, a firm which has purchased an asset at a lower price, will show a higher return, than the firm which has purchased the asset at a higher price.

5) **Change in Accounting Procedure:** Comparison between two variables prove worth provided their basis of valuation is identical. But in reality, it is not possible, such as methods of valuation of stock (FIFO or LIFO) or charging different methods of depreciation on fixed assets etc. Thus, if different methods are followed by different firms for their valuation, then comparison will practically be of no use.

6) **Qualitative Factors are ignored:** Ratios are tools of quantitative analysis only and normally qualitative factors which may generally influence the conclusions derived, are ignored while computing ratios. For instance, high current ratio may not necessarily mean sound liquid position when current assets includes a large inventory consisting of mostly obsolete items.

Therefore, it is very difficult to generalize whether a particular ratio is good or bad.

7) **Limited use of Single Ratio:** A single ratio would not be able to convey anything. Rations can be useful only when they are computed in a sufficient large number. If too many ratios are calculated, they are likely to confuse instead of revealing meaningful conclusions.

8) **Background is overlooked:** When inter-firm comparison is made, they differ substantially in age, size, nature of product etc. When an inter-firm comparison is made, these factors are not considered. Therefore, ratio analysis cannot give satisfactory results.

9) **Limited Use:** Ratio analysis is only a beginning and gives just a fraction of information needed for decision-making. Ratio analysis is not a substitute for sound judgment. But ratios are tools to aid in applying judgment. Conclusions drawn from the ratio analysis are not sure indicators of bad or good management. They merely convey certain observations which need further investigations, otherwise wrong conclusions may be drown. Computation of ratios is not useful unless they are interpreted.

10) **Personal Bias:** Ratios have to be interpreted and different people may interpret the same ratio in different ways. Ratios are only means of financial analysis but not an end in them. Ratios are simple to understand and easy to calculate. Therefore, there

is a tendency to over employ them. It should be clearly noted that ratios are only tools and the personal judgment of analyst is more important. The analyst has to carry further investigations and exercise his judgment in arriving at a correct diagnosis.

11) **Arithmetical Window Dressing:** Window–dressing means manipulation of accounts in a way so as to conceal vital facts and present the statements in a way to show better position than what it actually is. By doing so, it is possible to cover up bad financial position. Therefore, ratios based on such figures are not reliable.

12) **Changing Policies:** Ratios are computed on the basis of past result. Past is not an indicator of future. Ratios computed from historical data are used for predicting and projecting the likely events in the future. Such ratios may provide a glimpse of firm's past performance. But forecast for the future may not be correct as several other factors like management policies, market conditions etc. may induce future operations.

Ratios are only a post-mortem of what has happened between two Balance Sheet dates. The position in the interim period is not revealed by ratio analysis. Besides, they give no clue to future. Ratio analysis suffers from serious limitations. The analyst should not be carried away by its oversimplified nature, easy computation with a high degree of precision. They are as good as data itself.

The analyst must have comprehensive but practical knowledge and experience about the concerns whose statements have been used for calculating these rations. Ratios are not an end in themselves but they are means to achieve a particular end. Another limitation is that of standard ratio with which the actual rations may be compared. Generally, there is no such ratio which may be treated as standard for the purpose of comparison, because conditions of one concern differ significantly from those of another concern.

The analyst must be able to examine the nature of the data carefully. If accounting data lack uniformity particularly definitional uniformity, then ratios calculated on the basis of them will be misleading. Ratio analysis is one of the many techniques of analysis and interpretation. Thus, while attempting to draw any conclusion on this basis, other techniques should also be used.

4.8   INTERESTED PARTIES:

Ratio analysis of a firm's financial statements is of interest to a number of parties, mainly, share-holders, creditors, debtors, firm's own management etc. People in various walks of life are at present interested in ratio analysis though in different ways and fashion and each, however, from his own angle. The type of ratio analysis, its nature and dimension differ from party to party according to their objectives of financial analysis. Different ratios are used to signify different trends in the working of the firm. However, the table given below would help the students to have a rough idea. Parties interested and application of different ratios, in short, are given below:

INTERESTED PARTIES:

Parties Interested	Application of Ratios	To Test
I. Creditors (Short-term) Investors Money Lenders	Current Ratio Liquid Ratio Absolute Liquid Ratio Proprietary Ratio Assets to Proprietorship Ratio Debt-Equity Ratio Capital Gearing Ratio	Liquidity and Solvency
II. Share-holders Creditors (Long Term) Government Purchase of Enterprises Employees	Gross Profit Ratio Net Profit Ratio Operating Ratio Return of capital employed Dividend Ratio Earning per Share Dividend per Share	Profitability
III. Share-holders and Outsiders	Capital Gearing Ratio Equity Capital Ratio Long Term Loans to Net Worth	Capital Structure
IIII. Management	All types of ratios	Management Efficiency

4.9   CLASSIFICATION OF RATIOS:

Financial ratios have been classified in several ways. A number of standpoints may be used as base for classifying the ratios. It is a matter of great surprise that no uniformity has been achieved in the regard. Different authors have classified the ratios in varying groups. To illustrate, the short-term creditors' main interest is in the liquidity position or short-term solvency of the firm: long-term creditors are more interested in the long-term solvency and profitability analysis and the analysis of the firm's financial conditions; management is interested in evaluating every activity of the firm because they have to protect the interests of all parties. Thus accounting ratios may be classified on the following bases leading to somewhat overlapping categories.

(A) Classification by Statements:

The Traditional classification is based on those statements from which information is obtained for calculating the ratio. The ratios are classified as follows:

CLASSIFICATION BY STATEMENTS

Balance Sheet Ratios (Financial Ratios)	Profit & Loss A/c Ratios (Operating Ratios)	Inter-statement Ratios (Composite/Mixed Ratios)
Egs : Liquidity Ratio Current Ratio Stock Ratio Proprietary Ratio Debt-Equity Ratio Capital Gearing etc.	Egs : Gross Profit Ratio Net Profit Ratio Operating Ratio Expense Ratio etc.	Egs : Return on Capital Employed Return on Shareholders' Fund Turnover of Working Capital Debtors Turnover Ratio etc.

(B) Classification by Users:

This classification is based on the parties who are interested in making the use of ratios.

CLASSIFICATION BY USERS

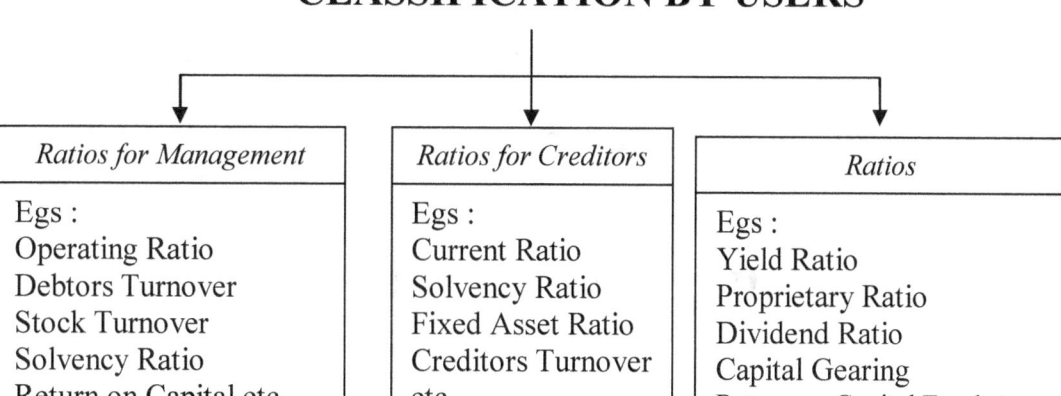

Ratios for Management	Ratios for Creditors	Ratios
Egs : Operating Ratio Debtors Turnover Stock Turnover Solvency Ratio Return on Capital etc.	Egs : Current Ratio Solvency Ratio Fixed Asset Ratio Creditors Turnover etc.	Egs : Yield Ratio Proprietary Ratio Dividend Ratio Capital Gearing Return on Capital Fund etc.

(C) <u>**Classification According to Importance:**</u>

This basis of classification of ratios has been recommended by the British Institute of Management. They are of two types.

CLASSIFICATION BY IMPORTANCE

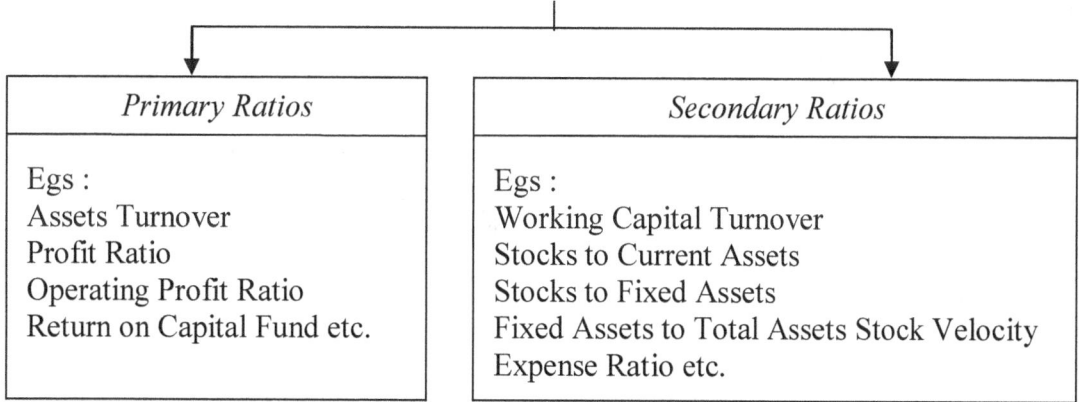

Primary Ratios	Secondary Ratios
Egs : Assets Turnover Profit Ratio Operating Profit Ratio Return on Capital Fund etc.	Egs : Working Capital Turnover Stocks to Current Assets Stocks to Fixed Assets Fixed Assets to Total Assets Stock Velocity Expense Ratio etc.

(D) <u>**Classification by Purpose/Function:**</u>

This is a classification based on the purpose for which an analyst computes these ratios. The modern approach of classifying the ratios is according to the purpose or object of analysis. Normally, ratios are used for the purpose of assessing the profitability and sound financial position. Thus, ratios according to the purpose are more meaningful. There can be several purposes which can be listed. For analysis, it is customary to group the purpose into broad headings. The following are the broad categories of accounting ratios from functional point of view:

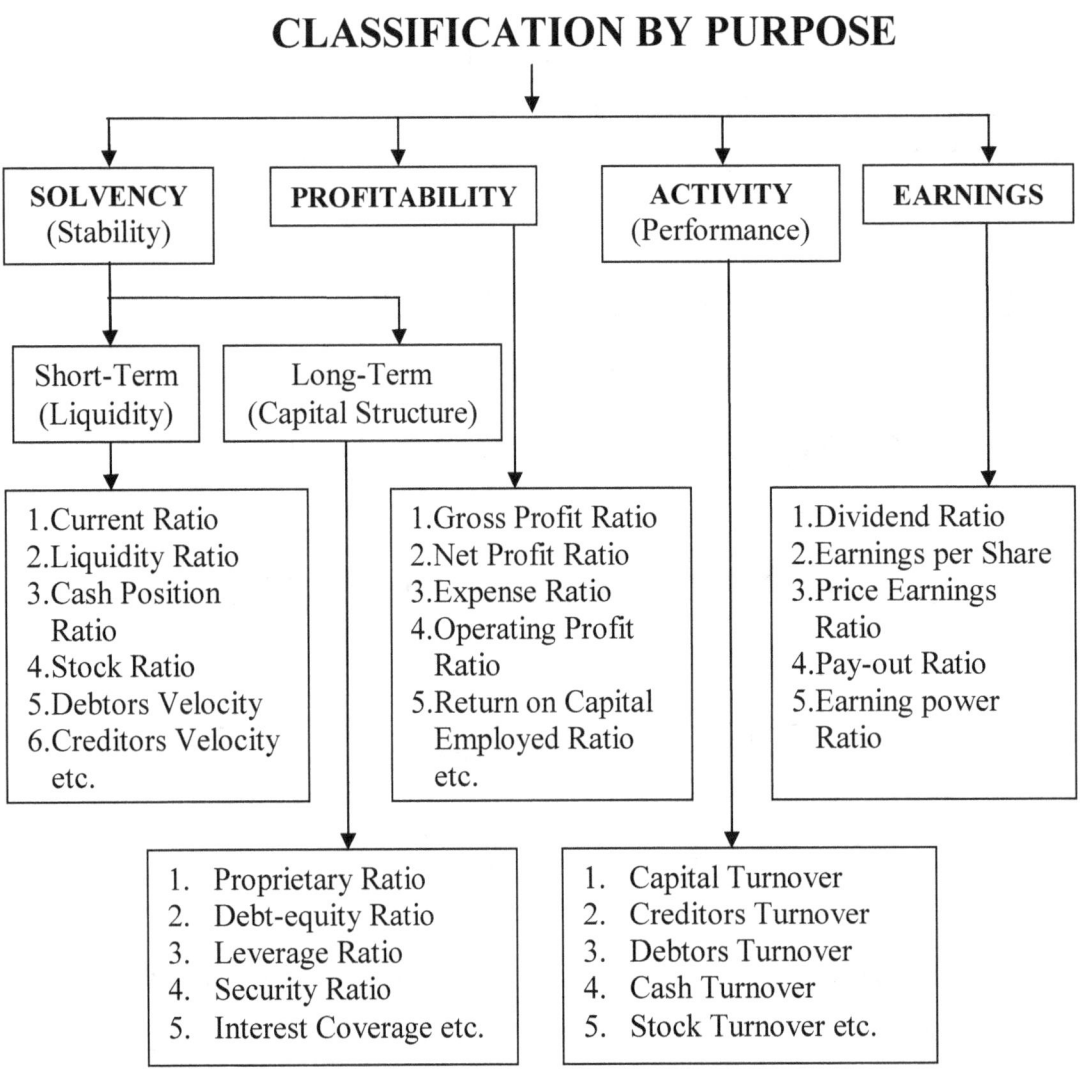

CLASSIFICATION BY PURPOSE

| SOLVENCY (Stability) | PROFITABILITY | ACTIVITY (Performance) | EARNINGS |

Short-Term (Liquidity)

Long-Term (Capital Structure)

1. Current Ratio
2. Liquidity Ratio
3. Cash Position Ratio
4. Stock Ratio
5. Debtors Velocity
6. Creditors Velocity etc.

1. Gross Profit Ratio
2. Net Profit Ratio
3. Expense Ratio
4. Operating Profit Ratio
5. Return on Capital Employed Ratio etc.

1. Dividend Ratio
2. Earnings per Share
3. Price Earnings Ratio
4. Pay-out Ratio
5. Earning power Ratio

1. Proprietary Ratio
2. Debt-equity Ratio
3. Leverage Ratio
4. Security Ratio
5. Interest Coverage etc.

1. Capital Turnover
2. Creditors Turnover
3. Debtors Turnover
4. Cash Turnover
5. Stock Turnover etc.

There are many types of classification of ratio. In this study researcher classified ration in four main part. They are liquidity ratios, capital structure ratios, profitability ratios and activity ratios. The brief descriptions are as under:

4.9.1 LIQUIDITY RATIOS:

The importance of adequate liquidity in the sense of the ability of a firm to meet current/short-term obligations when they become due for payment can hardly be overstressed. In fact, liquidity is a prerequisite for the very survival of a firm. The short-term creditors of the firm are interested in the short-term solvency or liquidity of the firm. But liquidity implies, from the viewpoint of utilisation of the funds of the firm that funds are idle or they earn very little. A proper balance between the two contradictory requirements, that is, liquidity and profitability, is required for efficient financial management. The liquidity ratios measure the ability of a firm to meet its short-term obligations and reflect the short-term financial strength/solvency of firm.

1) Current Ratio:

$$\text{Current Ratio} = \frac{\text{Current Assets}}{\text{Current Liabilities}} \times 100$$

Where as,

Current Assets = Cash in hand + Cash in bank + Debtors + Bills Receivable + Expenses + Money at call and short notice + Stock + Sundry Supplies + Other amounts receivable within a year.

Current Liabilities = Creditors + Bills Payable + bank overdraft + Expenses Outstanding + Interest Due of Payable + Reserve for Unbilled Expenses + Installment payable on long term-loansAny other amount which is payable within a year.

The current ratio of a firm measures its short-term solvency, that is, its ability to meet short-term obligations. As measure of short-term/current liquidity, it indicates the rupees of current assets available for each rupee of current liability/obligation payable. The bigger the current ratio, the larger is the amount of rupees available per rupee of current liability, the more is the firm's ability to meet current obligations and the greater is the safety of funds of short-term creditor.

4.9.2 CAPITAL STRUCTURE/LEVERAGE RATIO:

The second category of financial ratio is capital structure or leverage ratios. The long-term lender/creditors would judge the soundness of a firm on the basis of the long-term financial strength measured in terms of its ability to pay the interest regularly as we as repay the installment of principal on due dates or in one lump sum at the time of maturity. The long-term solvency of a firm can be examined by using leverage of capital structure ratios. The capital structure or leverage ratios may be defined as financial ratios which throw light on the long-term solvency of a firm as reflected in its ability to assure the long-term lenders with regard to (i) periodic payment of interest during the period of the loan and (ii) repayment of principal on maturity or in predetermined installments at due dates.

1) **Proprietary Ratio:**

Proprietary Ratio relates the proprietary funds to total assets. It is variant on the debt equity ratio. This ratio shows the long term or future solvency of the business. It is very important to creditors as it helps them to find out the proportion of proprietary fund in the total assets used in the business. Higher ratio indicates a secured position to creditors and a low ratio indicates greater risk to creditors.

$$\text{Proprietary Ratio} = \frac{\text{Proprietary Fund}}{\text{Total Assets}} \times 100$$

Where as,

Proprietary Fund = Preference Share Capital + Equity Share Capital + Reserve &surplus – Fictitious Assets.

Total Assets = Net Fixed Assets + Investments + Current Assets.

2) **Debt-Equity Ratios:**

The relationship between borrowed funds and owner's capital is a popular measure of the long-term financial solvency of a firm. This relationship is shown by the debt-equity ratios. This ratio reflects the relative claims of creditors and shareholders against the assets of the firm. Alternatively, this ratio indicates the relationship between outsider' claims and owner's capital can be shown in different ways and, accordingly, there are many variants of the debt-equity ratio.

One concept is to express the D/E ratio in terms of the relative proportion of long-term debt and shareholders' equity. Thus, The debt considered here is exclusive of current of current liabilities. The shareholders' equity includes (i) equity and preference share capital

(ii) past accumulated profit but excludes fictitious assets like past accumulated losses, (iii) discount on issues of shares and so on.

Another concept to the calculation of the debt-equity ratio is to relate the total debt (not merely long-term debt) to the shareholders' equity.

The D/E ratio is, thus the ratio of total outside liabilities to owners' total funds. In other words, it is ratio of the amount invested by outsiders to the amount invested by the owners of business.

Debt Equity Ratio (As per concept – 1):

$$= \frac{\text{Long term Debt}}{\text{Proprietary Fund}} \times 100$$

Debt Equity Ratio (As per concept – 1):

$$= \frac{\text{Total Debt}}{\text{Proprietary Fund}} \times 100$$

The difference between this and the first concept is essentially in respect of the treatment of current liabilities. While the former excludes them, the latter includes them in the numerator (debt).

4.9.3 PROFITABILITY RATIO

Apart from the creditors, both short-term and long-term, also interested in the financial soundness of a firm are the owners and management or the company itself. The management of the firm is naturally eager to measure its operating efficiency. Similarly, the owners invest their funds in the expectation of reasonable returns. The operating efficiency of a firm and its ability to ensure adequate returns to its shareholders/owners depends ultimately on the profits earned by it. The profitability ratios measure the profitability or the operational efficiency of the firm.

These ratios reflect the final results of business operations. The results of the firm can be evaluated in terms of its earnings with reference to a given level of assets or sales or owners interest etc. Therefore, the profitability ratios are broadly classified in three categories.

1)   Profitability ratios required for analysis from owners point of view.

2)   Profitability ratios based on Assets/Investments.

3)   Profitability ratios based on sales of the firm.

Profitability ratios required for analysis from owners point of view.

Return on equity, Earning per share, Dividend per share, Price earnings ratio are comes in this point of view.

In the KPT, there is no any share capital so that above stated ratio have not taken in this study.

Profitability ratios based on Assets/Investments:

1)   Return on Proprietors' Fund Ratio:

$$= \frac{\text{Net Profit}}{\text{Proprietors' Fund}} \times 100$$

Whereas,

Net Profit =   Net Profit after Tax.

Proprietors' Fund = Preference Share Capital + Equity Share Capital + Reserve & surplus – Fictitious Assets.

This ratio establishes profitability from the proprietors' point of view.

2) **Return on Capital Employed Ratio:**

$$= \frac{\text{Profit before Interest \& Tax}}{\text{Capital Employed}} \times 100$$

Whereas,

Capital Employed = Equity Share Capital + Preference Share Capital + Reserve and Surplus + Debenture and other Long-term debt – Fictitious assets.

This is also known as Return on Investment or Rate of Return. The prime objective of making investments in any business is to obtain satisfactory return on capital invested. It indicates the percentage of return of return on the capital in the business and it can be used to show the efficiency of the business as a whole.

A comparison of this ratio with similar firms, with the industry average and over time would provide sufficient insight into how efficiency the long-term funds of owners and creditors are being used. The higher the ratio, the more efficient use of the capital employed.

Profitability ratios based on sales of the firm:

3) **Gross Profit Ratio:**

$$= \frac{\text{Gross Profit}}{\text{Gross Income}} \times 100$$

Whereas,

Gross Profit and Gross income in Kandla Port Trust are as under:

Gross Profit =   Gross Income – Gross expenses.

Gross Income = Cargo handling & storage charges income + port & dock charges income.

Gross Expenses =   Cargo handling & storage charges expenses + port & dock charges expenses.

It is very useful as a test of profitability and management efficiency. It is generally contented that the margin of gross profit should be sufficient enough to recover all operating expenses and other expenses and also leave adequate amount as Net profit in relation to sales and owners' equity.

4)   Operating Profit Ratio:

$$= \frac{\text{Operating Profit}}{\text{Gross Income}} \times 100$$

Whereas,

Operating Profit and Gross income in Kandla Port Trust are as under:

Operating Profit = Operating Income - Operating Expenses.

Operating Income =   Cargo handling & storage charges income + port & dock charges income + Estate Rental + Township.

Operating Expenses = Cargo handling & storage charges expenses + port & dock charges expenses + Railway working + Rentable land & buildings + Management & general administrative expense + Township.

Gross Profit =   Gross Income – Gross expenses. (As Stated above)

It is very useful as a test of profitability and operating efficiency of the management.

5)   Net Profit Ratio:

$$= \frac{\text{Net Profit}}{\text{Gross Income}} \times 100$$

Whereas,

Net Profit =   Profit after Tax.

Gross Profit =   Gross Income – Gross expenses. (As Stated above)

It is also called Net Profit to Sales Ratio. The Net profit ratio is indicative of management's ability to operate the business with sufficient success not only recover from revenues of the period, the cost of merchandise or services, the expenses of operating the business and cost of borrowed funds, but also to leave a margin of reasonable compensation to the owners for providing their capital at risk. This ratio is used to measure the overall profitability and hence it is very useful to proprietors.

Expenses Ratio:

Another profitability ratio related to sales is the expense ratio. It becomes imperative to find out as how far the concern is able to save or is making over expenditure in respect of difference items of expenses. For this, relationship of each expense to incomes is established. Thus, these ratios reveal the relation of different expenses to income. It is computed by dividing expenses by income.

There are four main expenses to incomes ratios concerning to the KPT are as follows:

6) **Cargo Handling & Storage Charges Ratio:**

$$= \frac{\text{Cargo Handling \& Storage Charges Expenses}}{\text{Cargo Handling \& Storage Charges Income}} \times 100$$

7)Port& Dock Charges Ratio:

$$= \frac{\text{Port \& Dock Charges Expenses}}{\text{Port \& Dock Charges Income}} \times 100$$

8)Operating Expenses to Income Ratio:

$$= \frac{\text{Operating Expenses}}{\text{Operating Income}} \times 100$$

9) **Finance & Miscellaneous Expenses to Income Ratio:**

$$= \frac{\text{Finance \& Miscellaneous Expenses}}{\text{Finance \& Miscellaneous Income}} \times 100$$

4.9.4 ACTIVITY RATIO:

Activity ratios are concerned with measuring the efficiency in asset management. These ratios are also called efficiency ratios or asset utilisation ratios. The efficiency with which the assets are used would be reflected in the speed and rapidity with which assets are converted into sales. The greater is the rate of turnover or conversion, the more efficient is the utilisation of assets, other things being equal. For this reason, such ratios are also designated as turnover ratios. Turnover is the primary mode for measuring the extent of efficient employment of assets by relating the assets to sales. An activity ratio may, therefore, be defined as a test of the relationship between sales (more appropriately with cost of sales) and the various assets of a firm. Depending upon the various types of assets, there are various types of activity ratios.

Assets Turnover Ratio:

This ratio is known as the investment turnover ratio. It is based on the relationship between the cost of goods sold and investment of a firm. A reference to this was made while working out the overall profitability of a firm as reflected in its earning power. Depending upon the different concepts of assets employed, there are variants of this ratio.

1) **Fixed assets turnover ratio:**

$$= \frac{\text{Gross Income}}{\text{Net Fixed Assets}} \times 100$$

2) **Current assets turnover ratio:**

$$= \frac{\text{Gross Income}}{\text{Current Assets}} \times 100$$

Whereas,

Gross income = Cargo handling & storage charges income + port & dock charges income.

In this book for financial analysis we have chosen Kandla Post Trust as a case study. The Kandla Port Trust is a service-providing unit, so here all the asset turnover ratio is computed by dividing gross income by particular assets. Hence, the fixed assets are net of depreciation and the assets are exclusive of fictitious assets like debit balance of profit and loss account and deferred expenditures and so on.

The assets turnover ratio, howsoever defined, measures the efficient is the management and utilisation of the assets. The higher the turnover ratio, the more efficient is the management and utilisation of the assets while low turnover ratios are indicative of underutilization of available resources and presence of idle capacity.

CHAPTER – 05

DATA ANALYSIS

5.1   LIQUIDITY RATIOS:

5.1.1 CURRENT RATIO

$$= \frac{\text{Current Assets}}{\text{Current Liabilities}} \times 100$$

Table No. 5.1.1 Current Ratio

Years	Current Assets	Current Liabilities	Current Ratio (Times)
1999-2000	101913.62	9092.39	11.21:1
2000-2001	62885.19	6872.05	9.15:1
2001-2002	61999.67	5519.63	11.23:1
2002-2003	24824.31	5036.06	4.93:1
2003-2004	16255.78	7141.05	2.28:1
2004-2005	18943.01	9108.73	2.08:1
2005-2006	18102.16	10868.31	1.67:1
2006-2007	24573.17	16016.10	1.53:1
2007-2008	36140.40	27372.03	1.32:1
2008-2009	39367.03	17745.65	2.22:1
Minimum	16255.78	5036.06	1.32:1
Maximum	101913.62	27372.03	11.23:1
Average	40500.43	11477.20	4.76:1
Stand. Dev.	26093.67	6642.28	
Coefficient of Variation (C.V.)	64.43%	57.87%	

It can be seen from Table No. 5.1.1 that during the research period, minimum current ratio is reached at the stage of 1.32:1 in the year 2007-08 and maximum current ratio is reached at the stage of 11.23:1 in the year 2001-02.

The reason for minimum current ratio is that in the year 2007-08 current assets decreased by 10.77% and current liabilities increased by 138.49% compared to average current assets (40500.43) and current liabilities (11477.20). And also, in the year 2007-08 current liabilities have remained at the highest stage of 27372.03 lakhs during the entire research period.

The reason for maximum current ratio is that in the year 2001-02 current assets increased by 53.08% and current liabilities decreased by 51.91% compared to average current assets (40500.43) and current liabilities (11477.20).

As per Table No. 5.1.1, the Trust's average current ratio for the research period remained at 4.76:1. It shows that the Trust has maintained current assets of Rs.4.76 as compared to the current liabilities of Rs.1 during the study period.

It can be seen from Table No. 5.1.1, there are too many differences in minimum current ratio and maximum current ratio, because of that average current ratio could not be revealed actual average of the Trust. Initial four years' average current ratio is 9.13:1 and remained six years' current ratio is 1.85:1 of the study period. It shows the dispersion of average during the research period.

So that researcher has worked out standard deviation of current assets and current liabilities which were 26093.67 lakhs and 6642.28 lakhs for the study period. Standard deviation of current assets shows the dispersion of current assets of 26093.97 lakhs from the average current assets during the research period. Standard deviation of current liabilities shows the dispersion of current liabilities of 6642.28 lakhs from the average current liabilities during the research period.

For better understanding, researcher has also calculated Co-variance of current assets and current liabilities which were 64.43% and 57.87% for the study period. Co-variance of current assets shows the 64.43% instability in the current asset during the research period. Co-variance of current liabilities shows the 57.87% instability in the current liabilities during the research period.

It is apparent from Graph No.5.1.1 that there are too many fluctuations in the Current Ratio during the study period. The base year is 2002-03 in which the ratio is 4.93:1. Compared to the base year, the ratio has increased in the years 1999-2000 by 627.94%, in 2000-01 by 422.15% and in 2001-02 by 630.33%. After the base year, ratio has shown decreasing trend and compared to the base year it has decreased in the years 2003-04 by 265.29%, in 2004-05 by 284.97%, in 2005-06 by 326.37%, in 2006-07 by 339.50%, in 2007-08 by 360.90% and in 2008-09 by 271.09%.

5.2 CAPITAL STRUCTURE/LEVERAGE RATIO:

5.2.1 PROPRIETARY RATIO:

$$= \frac{\text{Proprietary Fund}}{\text{Total Assets}} \times 100$$

Table No. 5.2.1 Proprietary Ratio

Years	Proprietary Fund	Total Assets	Proprietary Ratio
1999-2000	145981.41	156891.98	93.05%
2000-2001	162260.00	170878.97	94.96%
2001-2002	180035.47	187245.27	96.15%
2002-2003	194140.38	200788.06	96.69%
2003-2004	203368.29	212120.96	95.87%
2004-2005	193053.75	203774.10	94.74%
2005-2006	212130.79	224610.72	94.44%
2006-2007	228128.68	245756.40	92.83%
2007-2008	249165.09	278148.74	89.58%
2008-2009	277584.33	296941.60	93.48%
Minimum	145981.41	156891.98	89.58%
Maximum	277584.33	296941.60	96.69%
Average	204584.82	217715.68	94.18%
Stand. Dev.	37415.95	42540.08	
Coefficient of Variation	18.29%	19.54%	
Coefficient of Correlation = r	0.9945		
Coefficient of Determination = r^2	0.9890		

It can be seen from Table No. 5.2.1 that during the research period minimum proprietary ratio is reached at the stage of 89.58% in the year 2007-08 and maximum proprietary ratio is reached at the stage of 96.69% in the year 2002-2003. There are no too many differences between maximum ratio and minimum ratio. The ratio rotates only in between 89.58% to 96.69%.

As per Table No. 5.2.1, the Trust's average proprietary ratio for the research period remained at 94.18%. It shows that in comparison to investment in total of Rs.100, the Trust has maintained of Rs.94.18 as proprietary fund during the period of research.

Standard deviation of proprietary fund and total assets remained low at 37415.95 lakhs and at 42540.08 lakhs during the research period. It shows the less dispersion from the average in proprietary fund and total assets during the period of study.

Covariance of proprietary fund and total assets remained only at 18.29% and at 19.54% during the research period. It indicates 81.71% (100 – 18.29) and 80.46% (100 – 19.54) stability in proprietary fund and total assets during the research period.

Let us also check the correlation between proprietary fund and total assets. For that, researcher has worked out coefficient of correlation and coefficient of determination which were 0.9945 and 0.9990 during the period of study.

Coefficient of correlation indicates that there is a high positive correlation between proprietary fund and total assets. Coefficient of determination revealed that 99.90% variation in proprietary fund is because of total assets and remaining only 0.10% variation is because of other factors. In other words, there too high effect of total assets on the proprietary fund and except total assets; other factors have effected very low on the proprietary fund during the research period.

It is apparent from Graph No. 5.2.1 that there is mix trend in the proprietary ratio during the study period. The base year is 2002-03 in which the ratio is 96.69%. The ratio of base year is stands on highest point of research period so that remaining year's ratio comes lower than the base year. For that, the ratio decreased in the years 1999-2000 by 3.64%, in 2000-2001 by 1.73%, in 2001-02 by 0.54%, in 2003-04 by 0.82%, in 2004-2005 by 1.95%, in 2005-06 by 2.25%, in 2006-07 by 3.86%, in 2007-08 by 7.11% and in 2008-09 by 3.21% comparing to the base the year.

Graph No. 5.2.1 PROPRIETARY RATIO

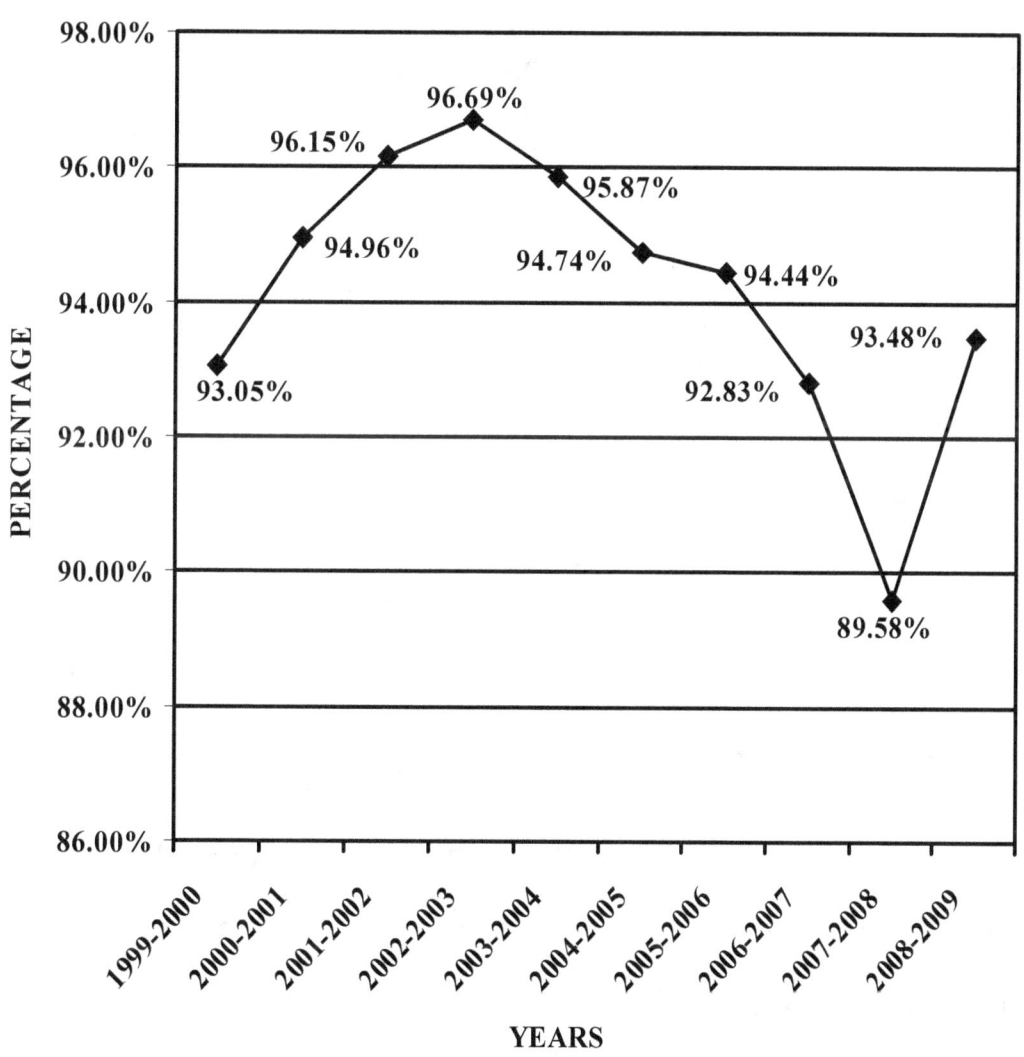

5.2.2 DEBT - EQUITY RATIO (As per Concept – 1)

$$= \frac{\text{Long term Debt}}{\text{Proprietary Fund}} \times 100$$

Table No. 5.2.2 Debt – Equity Ratio (As per Concept – 1)

Years	Long term Debt	Proprietary Fund	Debt - Equity Ratio
1999-2000	1818.19	145981.41	1.25%
2000-2001	1746.92	162260.00	1.08%
2001-2002	1690.17	180035.47	0.94%
2002-2003	1611.62	194140.38	0.83%
2003-2004	1611.62	203368.29	0.79%
2004-2005	1611.62	193053.75	0.83%
2005-2006	1611.62	212130.79	0.76%
2006-2007	1611.62	228128.68	0.71%
2007-2008	1611.62	249165.09	0.65%
2008-2009	1611.62	277584.33	0.58%
Minimum	1611.62	145981.41	0.58%
Maximum	1818.19	277584.33	1.25%
Average	1653.66	204584.82	0.84%
Stand. Dev.	70.34	37415.95	
Coefficient of Variation	4.25%	18.29%	
Coefficient of Correlation = r	-0.7508		
Coefficient of Determination = r^2	0.5637		

It can be seen from Table No. 5.2.2 that during the research period minimum debt equity ratio is reached at the stage of 0.58% in the year 2008-2009 and maximum debt equityratio is reached at the stage of 1.25% in the year 1999-2000.

The reason for minimum debt equity ratio is that in the year 2008-2009 long term debt decreased by 2.54% and proprietary fund increased by 35.68% compared to average long term debt (1653.66) and proprietary fund (204584.82). And also, in the year 2008-2009 long term debt has remained at the lowest point of 1611.62 lakhs where as proprietary fund has remained at the highest point of 277584.33 lakhs during the entire research period.

The reason for maximum debt equity ratio is that in the year 1999-2000 long term debt increased by 9.95% and proprietary fund decreased by 28.65% compared to average long term debt (1653.66) and proprietary fund (204584.82). And also, in the year 1999-2000 long term debt has remained at the highest point of 1818.19 lakhs whereas proprietary fund has remained at the lowest point of 145981.41 lakhs during the entire period of study.

As per Table No. 5.2.2, the Trust's average debt-equity ratio for the research period remained at 0.84%. It shows that when the investment by the Trust is of Rs.100, the investment by the outsiders is only of Rs.0.84 (i.e.84 paisa) into the total assets of Trust during the period of research.

Standard deviation of long term debt and proprietary fund remained very low at 70.35 lakhs and at 37415.95 lakhs during the research period. The reason of very low standard deviation of long term debt is that from the year 2002-2003 to 2008-2009 government loans remained same of Rs.1611.62 which is only one long term debt in the Trust. It shows the less dispersion from the average in long term debt and proprietary fund during the period of study.

Covariance of long term debt and proprietary fund remained only at 4.25% and at 18.29% during the research period. It indicates 95.75% (100 – 4.25) and 81.71% (100 – 18.29) stability in long-term debt and proprietary fund during the research period.

Let us also check the correlation between long term debt and proprietary fund. For that, researcher has worked out coefficient of correlation and coefficient of determination which were -0.7508 and 0.5637 during the period of study.

Coefficient of correlation indicates that there is a high negative correlation between long term debt and proprietary fund. Coefficient of determination revealed that 56.37% variation in long term debt is because of proprietary fund and remaining 43.63% variation is because of other factors. In other words, proprietary fund has affected only 56.37% to the long-term debt and except proprietary fund; other factors have affected 43.63% to the long-term debt during the research period.

It is apparent from Graph No.5.2.2 that the debt equity ratio remaining very low during the study period. The base year is 2002-03 in which the ratio is 0.83%. Compared to the base year, the ratio has increased in the years 1999-2000 by 0.42%, in 2000-01 by 0.25% and in 2001-02 by 0.11%. After the base year, ratio has gone down compared to the base year and it has decreased in the year 2003-04 by 0.04%, then, it is surprising that in the year 2004-05 ratio has remained as same as base year at 0.83%, then it shows decreasing trend and ratio continuously declined in the years 2005-06 by 0.07%, in 2006-07 by 0.12%, in 2007-08 by 0.18% and in 2008-09 by 0.25% compared to the base.

Graph No. 5.2.2 DEBT - EQUITY RATIO (As per Concept – 1)

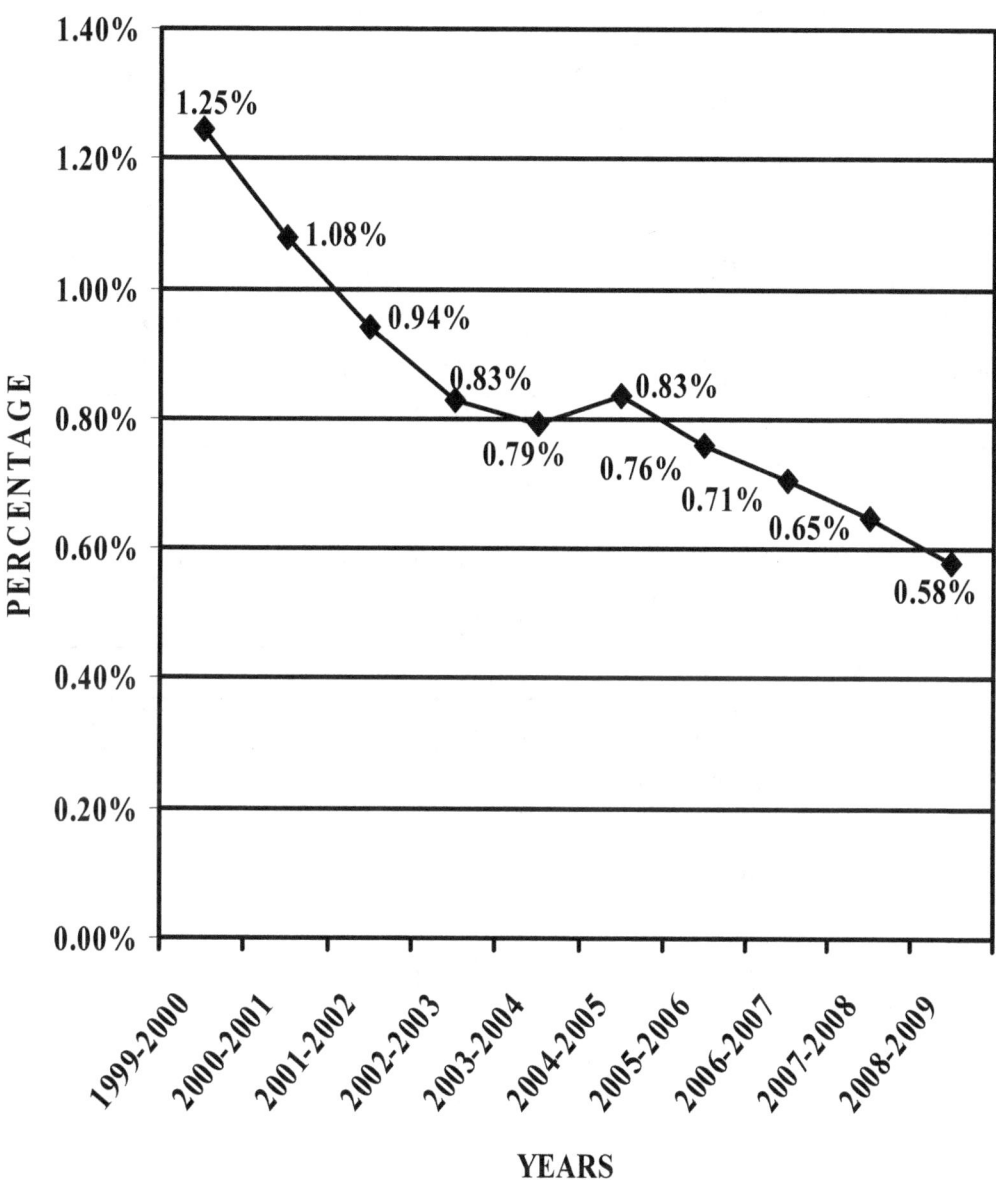

5.2.3 DEBT - EQUITY RATIO (As per Concept – 2)

$$= \frac{\text{Total Debt}}{\text{Proprietary Fund}} \times 100$$

Table No. 5.2.3 Debt – Equity Ratio (As per Concept – 2)

Years	Total Debt	Proprietary Fund	Debt - Equity Ratio
1999-2000	10910.58	145981.41	7.47%
2000-2001	8618.97	162260.00	5.31%
2001-2002	7209.79	180035.47	4.00%
2002-2003	6647.68	194140.38	3.42%
2003-2004	8752.67	203368.29	4.30%
2004-2005	10720.35	193053.75	5.55%
2005-2006	12479.93	212130.79	5.88%
2006-2007	17627.72	228128.68	7.73%
2007-2008	28983.65	249165.09	11.63%
2008-2009	19357.27	277584.33	6.97%
Minimum	6647.68	145981.41	3.42%
Maximum	28983.65	277584.33	11.63%
Average	13130.86	204584.82	6.23%
Stand. Dev.	6618.77	37415.95	
Coefficient of Variation	50.41%	18.29%	
Coefficient of Correlation = r	0.7387		
Coefficient of Determination = r^2	0.5457		

It can be seen from Table No. 5.2.3 that during the research period minimum debt equity ratio is reached at the stage of 3.42% in the year 2002-2003 and maximum debt equityratio is reached at the stage of 11.63% in the year 2007-2008.

The reason for minimum debt equity ratio is that in the year 2002-2003 total debt decreased by 49.37% whereas proprietary fund decreased only by 5.11% compared to average total debt (13130.86) and proprietary fund (204584.82). And also, in the year 2002-2003 total debt has remained at the lowest point of 6647.68 lakhs during the entire research period.

The reason for maximum debt equity ratio is that in the year 2007-2008 total debt increased by 120.73% whereas proprietary fund increased only by 21.79% compared to average total debt (13130.86) and proprietary fund (204584.82). And also, in the year 2007-2008 total debt has remained at the highest point of 28983.65 lakhs during the entire period of study.

As per Table No. 5.2.3, the Trust's average debt-equity ratio for the research period remained at 6.23%. It shows that when the investment by the Trust is of Rs.100, the investment by the outsiders is only of Rs.6.23 into the total assets of Trust during the period of research.

Standard deviation of total debt and proprietary fund was 6618.77 lakhs and 37415.95 lakhs during the research period. It shows the high dispersion from the average in total debt and low dispersion from the average in proprietary fund during the period of study.

Covariance of long term debt and proprietary fund was 50.41% and 18.29% during the research period. It indicates that 50.41% instability in total debt and 81.71% (100 – 18.29) stability in proprietary fund during the research period.

Let us also check the correlation between total debt and proprietary fund. For that, researcher has worked out coefficient of correlation and coefficient of determination which were 0.7387 and 0.5457 during the period of study.

Coefficient of correlation indicates that there is a high positive correlation between total debt and proprietary fund. Coefficient of determination revealed that 54.57% variation in total debt is because of proprietary fund and remaining 45.43% variation is because of other factors. In other words, proprietary fund has affected only 54.57% to the total debt and except proprietary fund; other factors have affected 45.43% to the total debt during the research period.

It is apparent from Graph No.5.2.3 that there is mix trend in the debt - equity ratio during the study period. The base year is 2002-03 in which the ratio is 3.42%. The ratio of base year is stands on lowest point of research period so that remaining year's ratio comes higher than the base year. For that, the ratio increased in the years 1999-2000 by 4.05%, in 2000-2001 by 1.89%, in 2001-02 by 0.58%, in 2003-04 by 0.88%, in 2004-2005 by 2.13%, in 2005-06 by 2.46%, in 2006-07 by 4.30%, in 2007-08 by 8.21% and in 2008-09 by 3.55% comparing to the base the year.

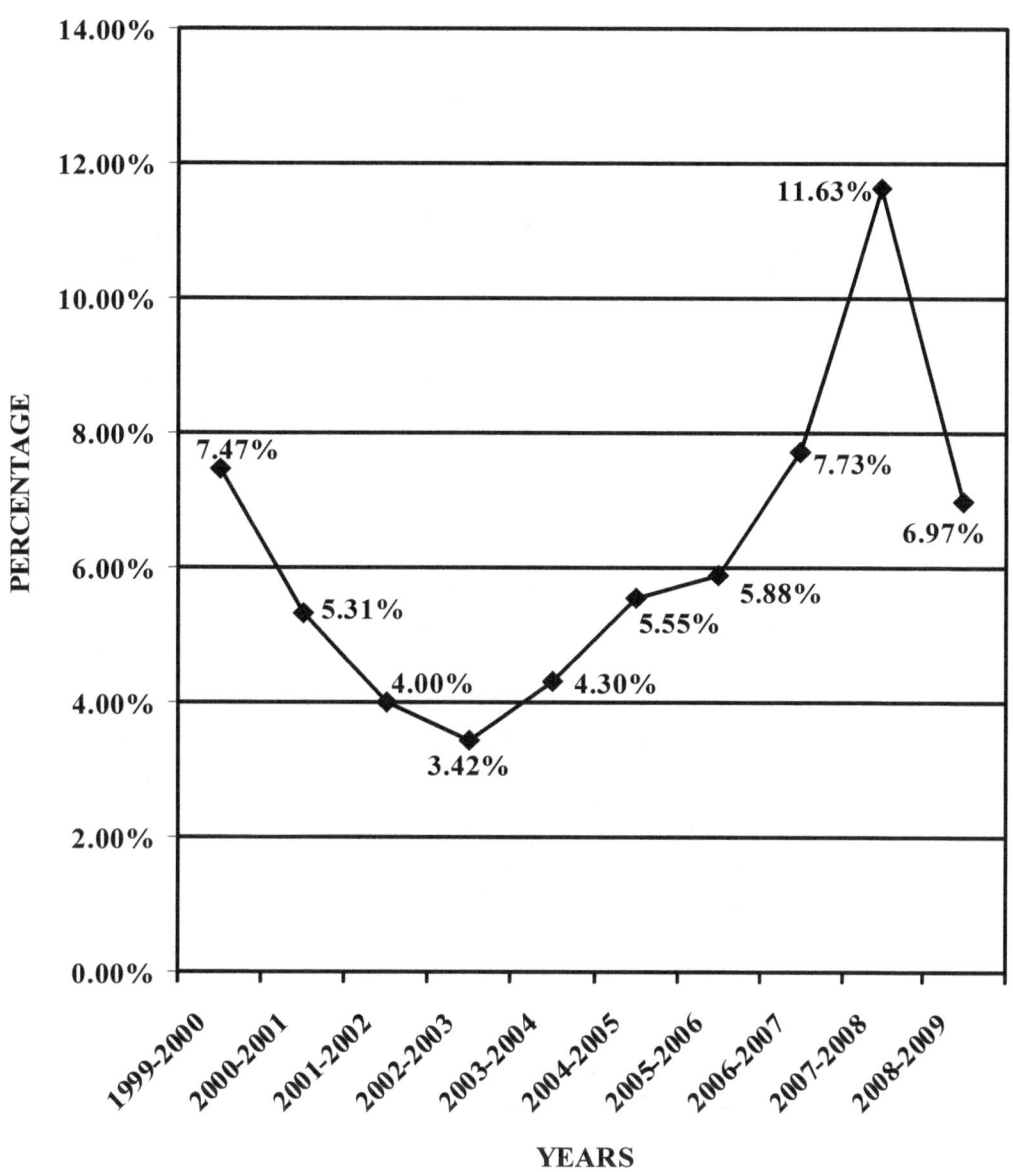

5.3 PROFITABILITY RATIO:

5.3.1 RETURN ON PROPRIETORS' FUND RATIO

$$= \frac{\text{Net Profit}}{\text{Proprietors' Fund}} \times 100$$

Table No. 5.3.1 Return on Proprietors' Fund Ratio

Years	Net Profit	Proprietors' Fund	Return on Proprietors' Fund Ratio
1999-2000	21491.59	145981.41	14.72%
2000-2001	17065.25	162260.00	10.52%
2001-2002	19240.19	180035.47	10.69%
2002-2003	14388.61	194140.38	7.41%
2003-2004	9063.08	203368.29	4.46%
2004-2005	19342.86	193053.75	10.02%
2005-2006	19072.55	212130.79	8.99%
2006-2007	15903.88	228128.68	6.97%
2007-2008	17786.99	249165.09	7.14%
2008-2009	16044.27	277584.33	5.78%
Minimum	9063.08	145981.41	4.46%
Maximum	21491.59	277584.33	14.72%
Average	16939.93	204584.82	8.67%
Stand. Dev.	3278.62	37415.95	
Coefficient of Variation	19.35%	18.29%	
Coefficient of Correlation = r	-0.2901		
Coefficient of Determination = r^2	0.0841		

It can be seen from Table No. 5.3.1 that during the research period minimum return on proprietors' fund ratio is reached at the stage of 4.46% in the year 2003-04 and maximum return on proprietors' fund ratio is reached at the stage of 14.72% in the year 1999-2000.

The reason for minimum return on proprietors' fund ratio is that in the year 2003-04 net profit decreased by 46.50% whereas proprietors' fund decreased only by 0.59% compared to average net profit (16939.93) and proprietors' fund (204584.82). And also, in the year 2003-04 net profit has remained at the lowest point of 9063.38 lakhs during the entire research period.

The reason for maximum return on proprietors' fund ratio is that in the year 1999-2000 net profit increased by 26.87% and proprietors' fund decreased by 28.65% compared to average net profit (16939.93) and proprietors' fund (204584.82). And also, in the year 1999-2000 net profit has remained at the highest stage of 21491.59 lakhs during the entire period of study.

As per Table No. 5.3.1, the Trust's average return on proprietors' fund ratio for the research period remained at 8.67%. It shows that the Trust can earn net profit of Rs.8.67 on each investment of Rs.100 in proprietors' fund during the research period.

Standard deviation of net profit and proprietors' fund remained low at 3278.62 lakhs and at 37415.95 lakhs during the research period. It shows the less dispersion from the average in net profit and proprietors' fund during the period of study.

Covariance of net profit and proprietors' fund remained at 19.35% and at 18.29% during the research period. It is indicated 80.65% (100 – 19.35) and 81.71% (100 – 18.29) stability in net profit and proprietors' fund during the research period.

Let us also check the correlation between net profit and proprietors' fund. For that, researcher has worked out coefficient of correlation and coefficient of determination which were -0.29 and 0.08 during the period of study.

Coefficient of correlation indicates that there is a low negative correlation between net profit and proprietors' fund. Coefficient of determination revealed that only 8.41% variation in net profit is because of proprietors' fund and remaining 91.59% variation is because of other factors. In simple words, there is very low effect of proprietors' fund on the net profit and except proprietors' fund; other factors have highly affected to the net profit during the research period.

It is apparent from Graph No. 5.3.1 that there are too many fluctuations in the return on proprietors' fund ratio during the study period. The base year is 2002-03 in which the ratio is 7.71%. Compared to the base year, the ratio has increased in the years 1999-2000 by 7.31%, in 2000-01 by 3.11% and in 2001-02 by 3.28%. After the base year, ratio has gone down compared to the base year and it has decreased in the years 2003-04 by 2.95%, then, it shows recovery in 2004-05 and 2005-06 and it increased by 2.61% and 1.58% respectively compared to the base year, then it shows decreasing trend and ratio continuously declined in the years 2006-07 by 0.44%, in 2007-08 by 0.27% and in 2008-09 1.63% compared to the base.

Graph No. 5.3.1 RETURN ON PROPRIETORS' FUND RATIO

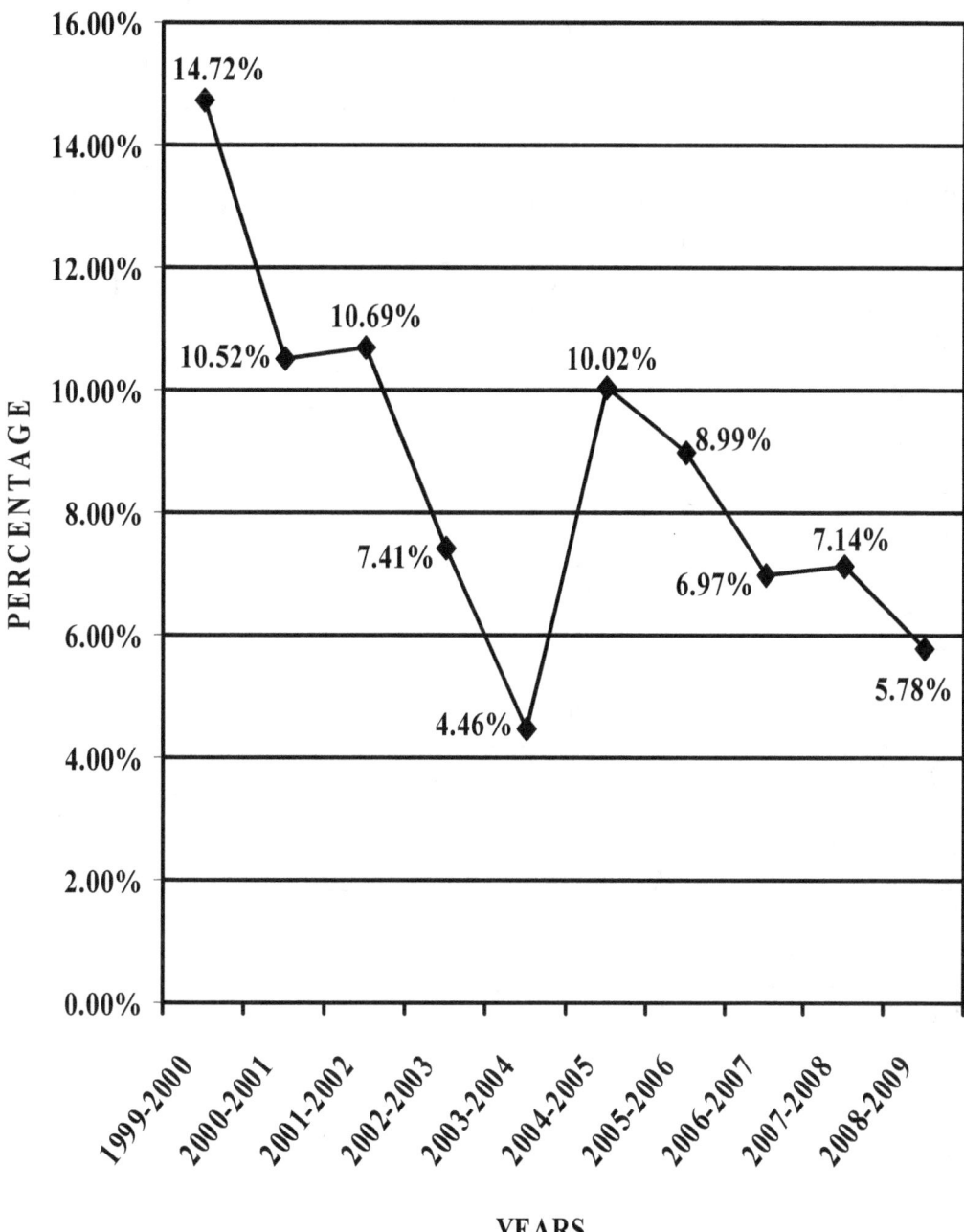

YEARS

5.3.2 RETURN ON CAPITAL EMPLOYED RATIO:

$$= \frac{\text{Profit before Interest \& Tax}}{\text{Capital Employed}} \times 100$$

Table No. 5.3.2 Return on Capital Employed Ratio

Years	Profit before Interest & Tax	Capital Employed	Return on Capital Employed Ratio
1999-2000	21467.53	147799.60	14.52%
2000-2001	17048.22	164006.91	10.39%
2001-2002	19229.18	181725.64	10.58%
2002-2003	17191.13	195752.00	8.78%
2003-2004	9048.08	204979.91	4.41%
2004-2005	19327.86	194665.37	9.93%
2005-2006	19986.27	213742.41	9.35%
2006-2007	21302.88	229740.30	9.27%
2007-2008	24693.75	250776.71	9.85%
2008-2009	22334.12	279195.95	8.00%
Minimum	9048.08	147799.60	4.41%
Maximum	24693.75	279195.95	14.52%
Average	19162.90	206238.48	9.51%
Stand. Dev.	4023.87	37363.17	
Coefficient of Variation	21.00%	18.12%	
Coefficient of Correlation = r	0.3450		
Coefficient of Determination = r^2	0.1190		

It can be seen from Table No. 5.3.2 that during the research period minimum return on capital employed ratio is reached at the stage of 4.41% in the year 2003-04 and maximum return on capital employed ratio is reached at the stage of 14.52% in the year 1999-2000.

The reason for minimum return on capital employed ratio is that in the year 2003-04 net profit decreased by 52.78% whereas capital employed decreased only by 0.61% compared to average profit before interest & tax (19162.90) and capital employed (206238.48). And also, in the year 2003-04 profit before interest & tax has remained at the lowest point of 9048.08 lakhs during the entire research period.

The reason for maximum return on capital employed ratio is that in the year 1999-2000 profit before interest & tax increased by 12.03% and capital employed decreased by 28.34% compared to average profit before interest & tax (19162.90) and capital employed (206238.48).

As per Table No. 5.3.2, the Trust's average return on capital employed ratio for the research period remained at 9.51%. It shows that the Trust can earn profit before interest & tax of Rs.9.57 on each investment of Rs.100 in capital employed during the research period.

Standard deviation of profit before interest & tax and capital employed remained low at 4023.87 lakhs and at 37367.17 lakhs during the research period. It shows the less dispersion from the average in profit before interest & tax and capital employed during the period of study.

Covariance of profit before interest & tax and capital employed remained only at 21.00% and at 18.12% during the research period. It indicates 79.00% (100 – 21.00) and 81.88% (100 – 18.12) stability in profit before interest & tax and capital employed during the research period.

Let us also check the correlation between profit before interest & tax and capital employed. For that, researcher has worked out coefficient of correlation and coefficient of determination, which were 0.3450 and 0.1190 during the period of study.

Coefficient of correlation indicates that there is a low positive correlation between profit before interest & tax and capital employed. Coefficient of determination revealed that 11.90% variation in profit before interest & tax is because of capital employed and remaining 88.10% variation is because of other factors. In other words, capital employed has an effect of only 11.90% to the profit before interest & tax; other factors have highly effect of 88.10% to the profit before interest & tax during the research period.

It is apparent from Graph No.5.3.2 that there is mix trend in the return on capital employed ratio during the study period. The base year is 2002-03 in which the ratio is 8.78%. The ratio of initial three years found to be higher than the base year while for last five years' ratio rotate nearby to the ratio of the base year. Compared to the base year, the ratio has increased in the years 1999-2000 by 5.74%, in 2000-01 by 1.68% and in 2001-02 by 1.80%. After the base year, ratio has moved out compared to the base year and it has decreased in the year 2003-04 by 4.37%, then, it shows little recovery in the years 2004-05 by 1.15%, in 2005-06 by 0.57%, in 2006-07 by 0.49% and 2007-08 by 1.06% compared to the base year, then again it declined in the year 2008-09 by 0.78% compared to the base.

Graph No. 5.3.2 RETURN ON CAPITAL EMPLOYED RATIO

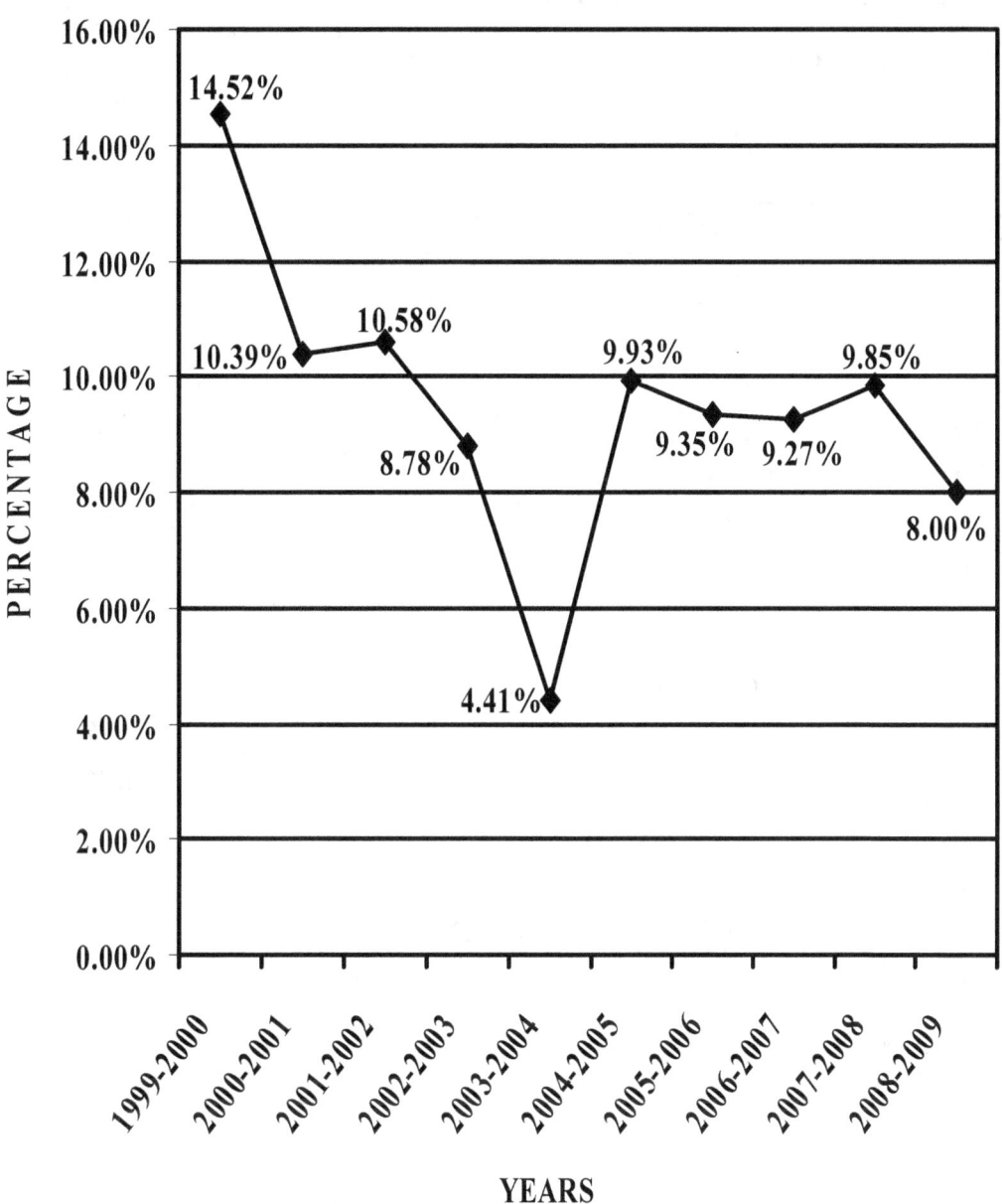

5.3.3 GROSS PROFIT RATIO:

$$= \frac{\text{Gross Profit}}{\text{Gross Income}} \times 100$$

Table No. 5.3.3 Gross Profit Ratio

Years	Gross Profit	Gross Income	Gross Profit Ratio
1999-2000	12018.63	21142.75	56.85%
2000-2001	9085.90	16500.44	55.06%
2001-2002	10403.39	16539.65	62.90%
2002-2003	10014.86	19439.51	51.52%
2003-2004	8405.18	19568.57	42.95%
2004-2005	9362.45	21119.14	44.33%
2005-2006	12023.10	23569.26	51.01%
2006-2007	14617.78	26975.69	54.19%
2007-2008	14461.54	32451.19	44.56%
2008-2009	14955.45	38731.21	38.61%
Minimum	8405.18	16500.44	38.61%
Maximum	14955.45	38731.21	62.90%
Average	11534.83	23603.74	50.20%
Stand. Dev.	2331.20	6816.89	
Coefficient of Variation	20.21%	28.88%	
Coefficient of Correlation = r	0.8593		
Coefficient of Determination = r^2	0.7384		

It can be seen from table No. 5.3.3 that during the research period minimum gross profit ratio is reached at the stage of 38.61% in the year 2008-09 and maximum gross profit ratiois reached at the stage of 62.90% in the year 2001-02.

The reason for minimum gross profit ratio is that in the year 2008-09 total gross expenses have remained at the highest point of 23775.76 lakhs during the entire study period.

The reason for maximum gross profit ratio is that in the year 2001-02 total gross expenses have remained at the lowest point of 6136.26 lakhs during the entire research period.

As per Table No. 5.3.3, the Trust's average gross profit ratio for the research period remained at 50.20%. It shows that the Trust can earn gross profit of Rs.50.20 on the gross income of Rs.100 which states that the net gross expense is of Rs.49.80 during the research period.

It can be seen that during the period of study there has not been much fluctuation in the ratio. Ratio remained nearby to the average ratio, throughout the research period. It shows the stability in gross profit ratio. The reasons for stability in gross profit ratio as follows:

⇒ Standard deviation of gross profit and gross income remained low at 2331.20 lakhs and at 6816.89 lakhs during the research period. It shows the less dispersion from the average in gross profit and gross income during the period of study.

⇒ Covariance of gross profit and gross income remained only at 20.21% and at 28.88% during the research period. It indicates 79.79% (100 - 20.21) and 71.12% (100 - 28.88) stability in gross profit and gross income during the research period.

Let us also check the correlation between gross profit and gross income. For that, researcher has worked out coefficient of correlation and coefficient of determination which were 0.8593 and 0.7384 during the period of study.

Coefficient of correlation indicates that there is high positive correlation between gross profit and gross income. Coefficient of determination revealed that 73.84% variation in gross profit is because of gross income and remaining 26.16% variation is because of other factors. In other words, gross income has an effect of 73.84% on the gross profit and except gross income; other factors have an effect of 26.16% on the gross profit during the research period.

It is apparent from Graph No. 5.3.3 that there is mixed trend in the gross profit ratio during the study period. The base year is 2002-03 in which the ratio is 51.52%. Compared to the base year, the ratio has increased in the years 1999-2000 by 5.33%, in 2000-01 by 3.55% and in 2001-02 by 11.38%. After the base year, ratio has gone down compared to the base year and it has decreased in the years 2003-04 by 8.57%, in 2004-05 by 7.19% and in 2005-06 by 0.51%, then, it shows a little recovery in 2006-07 and it increased by 2.67% compared to the base year, then again it decreased in 2007-08 by 6.95% and in 2008-09 it shows the highest decrease by 12.90% compared to the base year during the period of study.

Graph No. 5.3.3 GROSS PROFIT RATIO

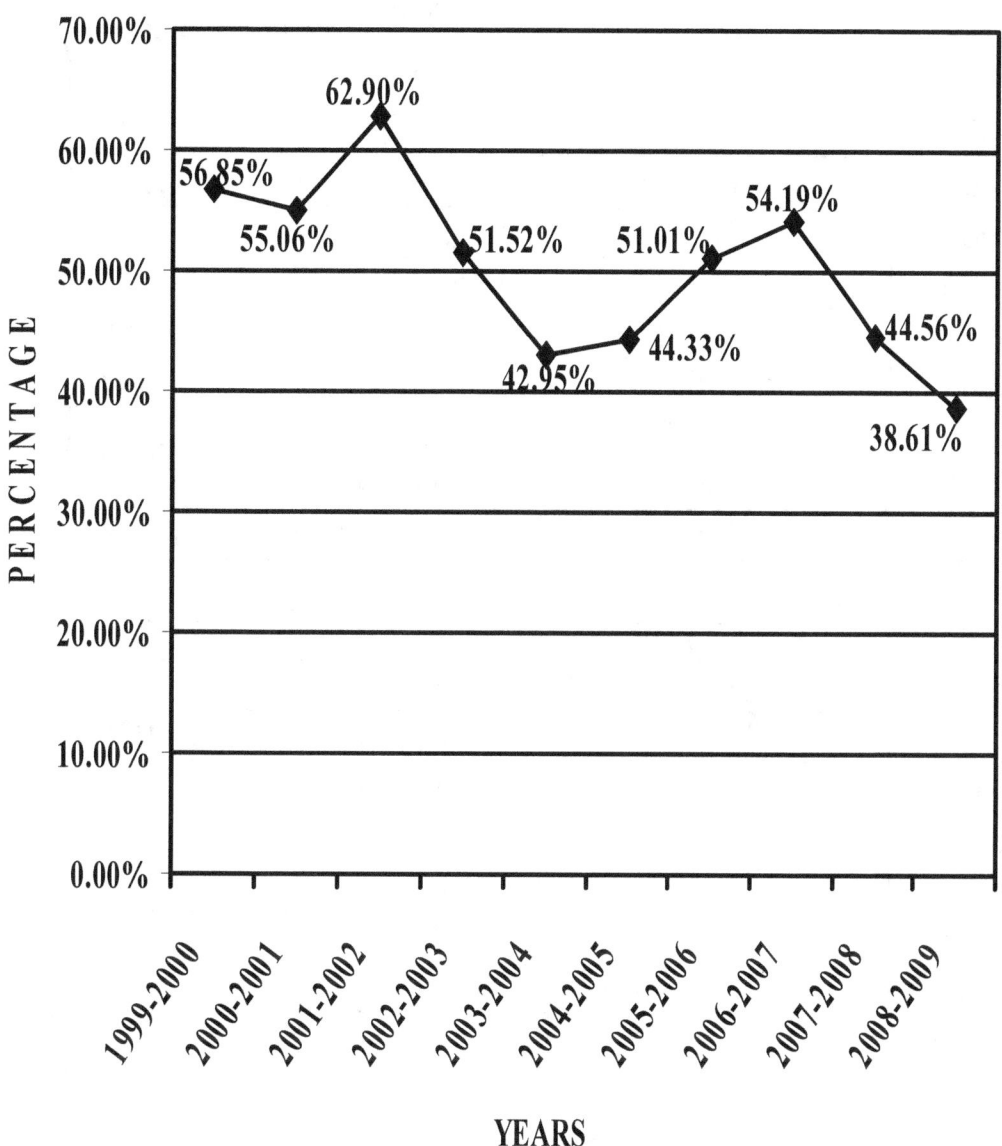

5.3.4 OPERATING PROFIT RATIO:

$$= \frac{\text{Operating Profit}}{\text{Gross Income}} \times 100$$

Table No. 5.3.4 Operating Profit Ratio

Years	Operating Profit	Gross Income	Operating Profit Ratio
1999-2000	9877.23	21142.75	46.72%
2000-2001	6557.93	16500.44	39.74%
2001-2002	7471.71	16539.65	45.17%
2002-2003	7225.66	19439.51	37.17%
2003-2004	4534.09	19568.57	23.17%
2004-2005	6348.20	21119.14	30.06%
2005-2006	8130.54	23569.26	34.50%
2006-2007	11488.74	26975.69	42.59%
2007-2008	9360.39	32451.19	28.84%
2008-2009	8229.80	38731.21	21.25%
Minimum	4534.09	16500.44	21.25%
Maximum	11488.74	38731.21	46.72%
Average	7922.43	23603.74	34.92%
Stand. Dev.	1877.63	6816.89	
Coefficient of Variation	23.70%	28.88%	
Coefficient of Correlation = r	0.4527		
Coefficient of Determination = r^2	0.2049		

It can be seen from Table No. 5.3.4 that during the research period minimum operating profit ratio is reached at the stage of 21.25% in the year 2008-09 and maximum operating profit ratiois reached at the stage of 46.72% in the year 1999-00.

The first reason for minimum operating profit ratio is that in the year 2008-09 total operating expenses were remained at the highest point of 32646.09 lakhs during the entire study period. The second reason for minimum operating profit ratio is that in that year gross income increased by 64.09% compared to average gross income (23603.74).

The reason for maximum operating profit ratio is that in the year 1999-2000 operating profit increased by 24.67% and gross income decreased by 10.43% compared to average operating profit (7922.43) and gross income (23603.74).

As per Table No. 5.3.4, the Trust's average operating profit ratio for the research period remained at 34.92%. It shows that the Trust can earn operating profit of Rs.34.92 on the gross income of Rs.100, which states that the net operating expense is of Rs.65.08 during the research period.

During the research period, there are seen ups and downs in the operating profit ratio. In the years 1999-2000, 2001-02 and 2007-08 ratio remained too high to the average at the stage of 46.72%, 45.17% and 42.59% respectively and in the years 2003-04 and 2008-09 ratio remained too low to the average at the stage of 23.07% and 23.17%. While in remaining years, ration routed nearby to the average. So that standard deviation and covariance were come low.

Standard deviation of operating profit and gross income remained low at 1877.63 lakhs and at 6816.89 lakhs during the research period. It shows the less dispersion from the average in operating profit and gross income during the period of study.

Covariance of operating profit and gross income remained only at 23.70% and at 28.88% during the research period. It indicates

76.30% (100 - 23.70) and 71.12% (100 - 28.88) stability in operating profit and gross income during the research period.

Let us also check the correlation between operating profit and gross income. For that, researcher has worked out coefficient of correlation and coefficient of determination which were 0.4527 and 0.2049 during the period of study.

Coefficient of correlation indicates that there is low positive correlation between operating profit and gross income. Coefficient of determination revealed that 20.49% variation in operating profit is because of gross income and remaining 79.51% variation is because of other factors. In other words, gross income has an effect of only 20.49% on the operating profit and except gross income; other factors have an effect of 79.51% on the operating profit during the research period.

It is apparent from Graph No. 5.3.4 that there is flexible trend in the operating profit ratio during the study period. The base year is 2002-03 in which the ratio is 37.17%. Compared to the base year, the ratio has increased in the years 1999-2000 by 9.55%, in 2000-01 by 2.57% and in 2001-02 by 8.00%. After the base year, ratio has gone down compared to the base year and it has decreased in the years 2003-04 by 14.00%, in 2004-05 by 7.11% and in 2005-06 by 2.67, then, it shows little recovery in 2006-07 and it increased by 5.42% compared to the base year, then again it decreased in 2007-08 by 8.33% and in 2008-09 it shows the highest decline by 15.92% compared to the base year during the period of study.

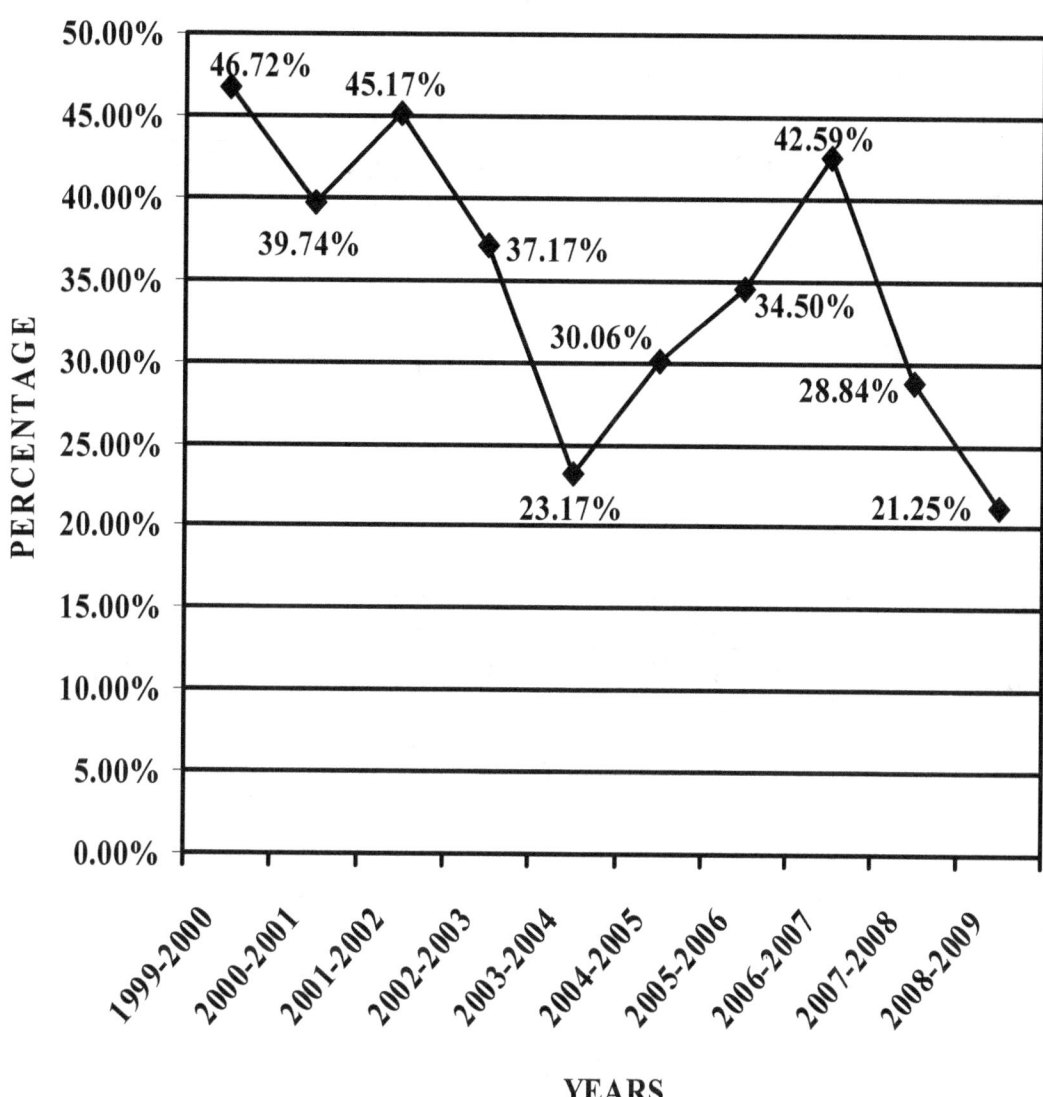

Graph No. 5.3.4 OPERATING PROFIT RATIO

5.3.5 NET PROFIT RATIO:

$$= \frac{\text{Net Profit}}{\text{Gross Income}} \times 100$$

Table No. 5.3.5 Net Profit Ratio

Years	Net Profit	Gross Income	Net Profit Ratio
1999-2000	21491.59	21142.75	101.65%
2000-2001	17065.25	16500.44	103.42%
2001-2002	19240.19	16539.65	116.33%
2002-2003	14388.61	19439.51	74.02%
2003-2004	9063.08	19568.57	46.31%
2004-2005	19342.86	21119.14	91.59%
2005-2006	19072.55	23569.26	80.92%
2006-2007	15903.88	26975.69	58.96%
2007-2008	17786.99	32451.19	54.81%
2008-2009	16044.27	38731.21	41.42%
Minimum	9063.08	16500.44	41.42%
Maximum	21491.59	38731.21	116.33%
Average	16939.93	23603.74	76.94%
Stand. Dev.	3278.62	6816.89	
Coefficient of Variation	19.35%	28.88%	
Coefficient of Correlation = r	-0.0068		
Coefficient of Determination = r^2	0.000046		

It can be seen from Table No. 5.3.5 that during the research period minimum net profit ratio is reached at the stage of 41.42% in the year 2008-09 and maximum net profit ratio is reached at the stage of 116.33% in the year 2001-02.

The reason for minimum net profit ratio is that in the year 2008-09 net profit decreased by 5.29% and gross income increased by 64.09% compared to average net profit (16939.93) and gross income

(23603.74). And also, in the year 2008-09 gross income has remained at the highest point of 38731.31 lakhs during the entire research period.

The reason for maximum net profit is that in the year 2001-02 net profit increased by 13.58% and gross income decreased by 29.93% compared to average net profit (16939.93) and gross income (23603.74).

As per Table No. 5.3.5, the Trust's average net profit ratio for the research period remained at 76.94%. It shows that the Trust can earn net profit of Rs.76.94 from the gross income of Rs.100 during the research period.

It can be seen from Table No. 5.3.5, there are too many differences in minimum net profit ratio and maximum net profit ratio, because of that average net profit ratio could not be revealed actual average of the Trust. Initial three years' average net profit ratio is 107.13% and remained seven years' net profit ratio is 64.00% of the study period. It shows the dispersion of average during the research period.

So that researcher has worked out standard deviation of net profit and gross income which were 3278.62 lakhs and 6816.89 lakhs for the study period. Standard deviation of net profit shows the dispersion of net profit of 3278.62 lakhs from the average net profit during the research period. Standard deviation of gross income shows the dispersion of gross income of 6816.89 lakhs from the average gross income during the research period.

For better understanding, researcher has also calculated Co-variance of net profit and gross income which were 19.35% and 28.88% for the study period. Co-variance of net profit shows the 19.35% instability in the net profit during the research period. Co-variance of gross income shows the 28.88% instability in the gross income during the research period.

Let us also check the correlation between operating profit and gross income. For that, researcher has worked out coefficient of correlation and coefficient of determination which were -0.0068 and 0.000046 during the period of study.

Coefficient of correlation indicates that there is a very low negative correlation between net profit and gross income. Coefficient of determination revealed that only 0.0046% variation in net profit is because of gross income and remaining 99.9954% variation is because of other factors. In simple words, there is very low effect of gross income on the net profit and except gross income; other factors have highly affected to the net profit during the research period.

It is apparent from Graph No.5.3.5 that there is mix trend in the net profit ratio during the study period. The base year is 2002-03 in which the ratio is 74.02%. Compared to the base year, the ratio has increased in the years 1999-2000 by 27.63%, in 2000-01 by 29.41% and in 2001-02 by 42.31%. After the base year, ratio has gone down compared to the base year and it has decreased in the years 2003-04 by 27.70%, then, it shows recovery in 2004-05 and 2005-06 and it increased by 17.57% and 6.90% respectively compared to the base year, then it shows decreasing trend and ratio continuously declined in the years 2006-07 by 15.06%, in 2007-08 by19.21% and in 2008-09 it shows the highest decline by 32.59% compared to the base year during the period of study.

Graph No. 5.3.5 NET PROFIT RATIO

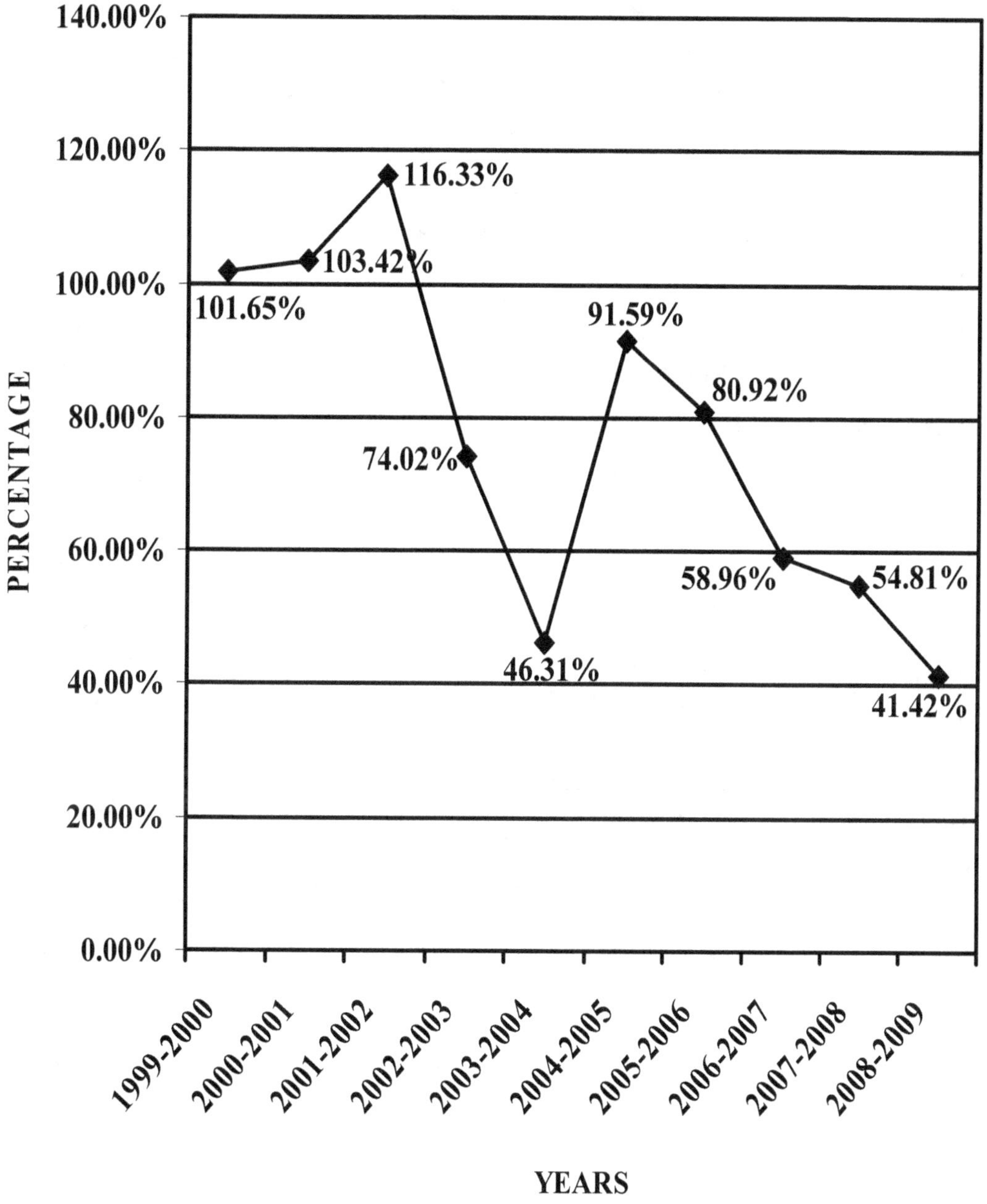

5.3.6 CARGO HANDLING & STORAGE CHARGES RATIO:

$$= \frac{\text{Cargo Handling \& Storage Charges Expenses}}{\text{Cargo Handling \& Storage Charges Income}} \times 100$$

Table No. 5.3.6 Cargo Handling & Storage Charges Ratio

Years	Cargo Handling & Storage Charges Expenses	Cargo Handling & Storage Charges Income	Cargo Handling & Storage Charges Ratio
1999-2000	2300.83	11304.12	20.35%
2000-2001	2317.14	8086.87	28.65%
2001-2002	2432.25	7975.54	30.50%
2002-2003	2671.62	9040.16	29.55%
2003-2004	3012.85	9444.47	31.90%
2004-2005	3402.29	10489.39	32.44%
2005-2006	3609.03	12867.06	28.05%
2006-2007	3748.51	13544.97	27.67%
2007-2008	6891.63	18141.54	37.99%
2008-2009	8279.17	19814.27	41.78%
Minimum	2300.83	7975.54	20.35%
Maximum	8279.17	19814.27	41.78%
Average	3866.53	12070.84	30.89%
Stand. Dev.	1948.95	3891.48	
Coefficient of Variation	50.41%	32.24%	
Coefficient of Correlation = r	0.9493		
Coefficient of Determination = r^2	0.9012		

It can be seen from Table No. 5.3.6 that during the research period minimum cargo handling & storage charges ratio is reached at the stage of 20.35% in the year 1999-2000 and maximum cargo handling & storage charges ratio is reached at the stage of 41.78% in the year 2008-2009.

The reason for minimum cargo handling & storage charges ratio is that in the year 1999-2000 cargo handling & storage charges expenses decreased by 40.49% whereas cargo handling & storage charges income decreased by 6.35% compared to average cargo handling & storage charges expenses (3866.33) and cargo handling & storage charges income (12070.84). And also, in the year 1999-2000 cargo handling & storage charges expenses have remained at the lowest point of 2300.83 lakhs during the entire research period.

The reason for maximum cargo handling & storage charges ratio is that in the year 2008-2009 cargo handling & storage charges expenses is highly increased by 114.12% whereas cargo handling & storage charges income increased by 64.15% compared to average cargo handling & storage charges expenses (3866.33) and cargo handling & storage charges income (12070.84). And also, in the year 2008-2008 cargo handling & storage charges expenses and cargo handling & storage charges income have remained at the highest point of 8279.17 lakhs and 19814.27 lakhs during the entire period of study.

As per Table No. 5.3.6, the Trust's average cargo handling & storage charges ratio for the research period remained at 30.89%. It shows that the Trust spends cargo handling & storage charges expenses of Rs.30.89 to earn cargo handling & storage charges income of Rs.100, which states that the trust has earned the net cargo handling & storage charges income of Rs.69.11 during the research period.

Standard deviation of cargo handling & storage charges expenses and cargo handling & storage charges income remained at 1948.95 lakhs and at 3891.48 lakhs during the research period. It shows the dispersion from the average in cargo handling & storage charges expenses and cargo handling & storage charges income during the period of study.

Covariance of cargo handling & storage charges expenses and cargo handling & storage charges income remained at 50.41% and at 32.24% during the research period. It indicates 50.41% and 32.24% instability in cargo handling & storage charges expenses and cargo handling & storage charges income during the period of research.

Let us also check the correlation between cargo handling & storage charges expenses and cargo handling & storage charges income. For that, researcher has worked out coefficient of correlation and coefficient of determination which were 0.9493 and 0.9012 during the period of study.

Coefficient of correlation indicates that there is a high positive correlation between cargo handling & storage charges expenses and cargo handling & storage charges income. Coefficient of determination revealed that 90.12% variation in cargo handling & storage charges expenses is because of cargo handling & storage charges income and remaining 9.88% variation is because of other factors. In other words, cargo handling & storage charges income has affected 90.12% to the cargo handling & storage charges expenses and except cargo handling & storage charges income; other factors have affected 9.88% to cargo handling & storage charges expenses during the research period.

It is apparent from Graph No.5.3.6 that there is fluctuating trend in the cargo handling & storage charges ratio during the study period. The base year is 2002-03 in which the ratio is 29.55%. Compared to the base year, the ratio has decreased in the years 1999-2000 by 9.20% and in 2000-2001 by 0.90%, then, it has increased in the years 2001-02 by 0.94%, in 2003-04 by 2.35% and in 2004-05 by 2.88% compared to the base year, then again it has shown decline in the years 2005-06 by 1.50% and in 2006-07 by 1.88% compared to the base year, then again it has increased in the years 2007-08 by 8.14% and in 2008-09 by 12.23% compared to the base year.

Graph No. 5.3.6 CARGO HANDLING & STORAGE CHARGES RATIO

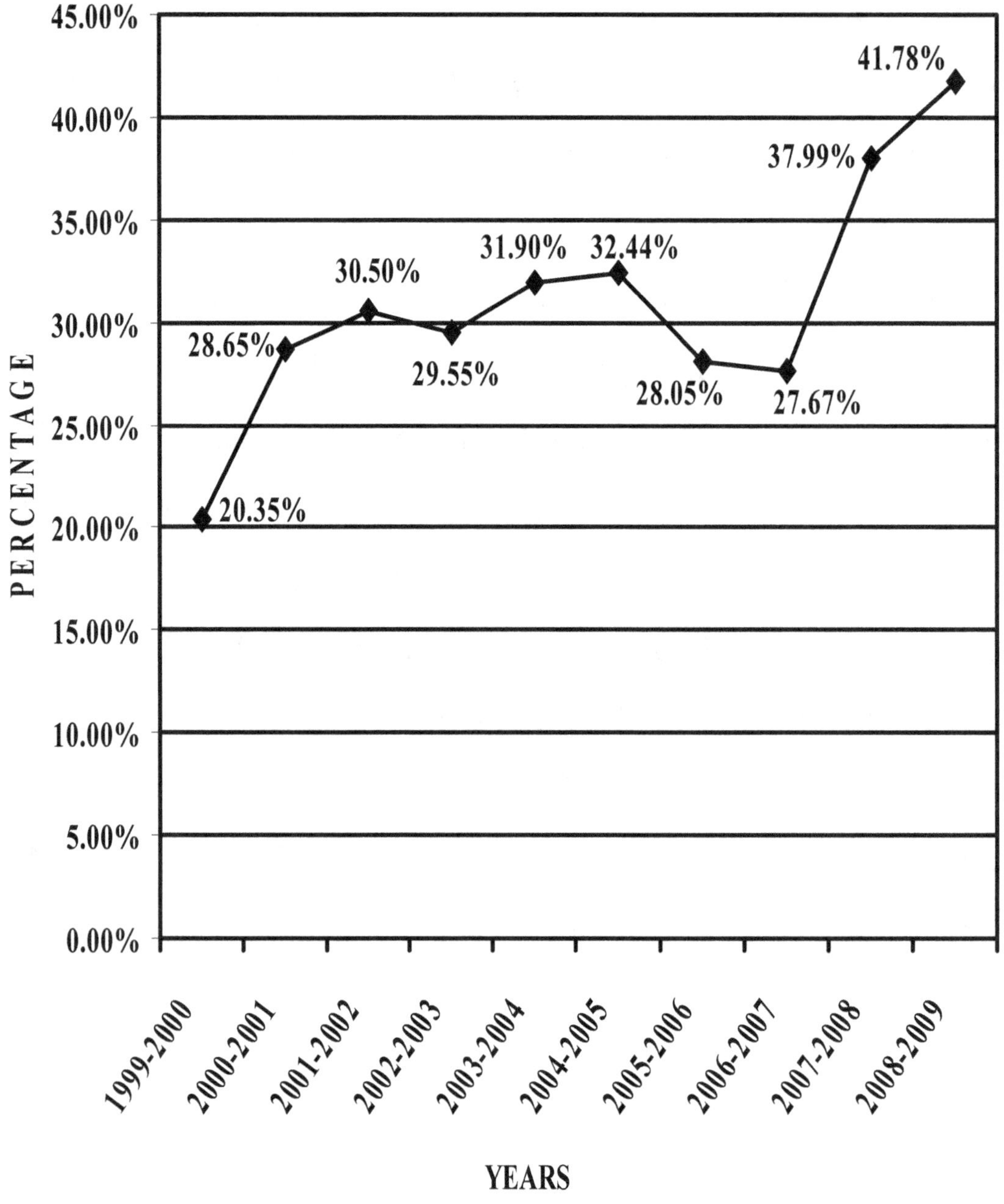

The chart shows PERCENTAGE on the y-axis (ranging from 0.00% to 45.00%) and YEARS on the x-axis.

Data points:
- 1999-2000: 20.35%
- 2000-2001: 28.65%
- 2001-2002: 30.50%
- 2002-2003: 29.55%
- 2003-2004: 31.90%
- 2004-2005: 32.44%
- 2005-2006: 28.05%
- 2006-2007: 27.67%
- 2007-2008: 37.99%
- 2008-2009: 41.78%

5.3.7 PORT & DOCK CHARGES RATIO:

$$= \frac{\text{Port \& Dock Charges Expenses}}{\text{Port \& Dock Charges Income}} \times 100$$

Table No. 5.3.7 Port & Dock Charges Ratio

Years	Port & Dock Charges Expenses	Port & Dock Charges Income	Port & Dock Charges Ratio
1999-2000	6823.29	9838.63	69.35%
2000-2001	5097.40	8413.57	60.59%
2001-2002	3704.01	8564.11	43.25%
2002-2003	6753.03	10399.35	64.94%
2003-2004	8150.54	10124.10	80.51%
2004-2005	8354.40	10629.75	78.59%
2005-2006	7937.13	10702.20	74.16%
2006-2007	8609.40	13430.72	64.10%
2007-2008	11098.02	14309.65	77.56%
2008-2009	15496.59	18916.94	81.92%
Minimum	3704.01	8413.57	43.25%
Maximum	15496.59	18916.94	81.92%
Average	8202.38	11532.90	69.50%
Stand. Dev.	3094.04	3033.58	
Coefficient of Variation	37.72%	26.30%	
Coefficient of Correlation = r	0.9573		
Coefficient of Determination $= r^2$	0.9164		

It can be seen from Table No. 5.3.7 that during the research period minimum port & dock charges ratio is reached at the stage of 43.25% in the year 2001-2002 and maximum port & dock charges ratio is reached at the stage of 81.92% in the year 2008-2009.

The reason for minimum port & dock charges ratio is that in the year 2001-2002 port & dock charges expenses decreased by 54.84% and port & dock charges income decreased by 25.74% compared to average port & dock charges expenses (8202.38) and port & dock charges income (11532.90). And also, in the year 2001-2002 port & dock charges expenses have remained at the lowest point of 3704.01 lakhs during the entire research period.

The reason for maximum port & dock charges ratio is that in the year 2008-2009 port & dock charges expenses is highly increased by 88.93% whereas port & dock charges income increased by 64.03% compared to average port & dock charges expenses (8202.38) and port & dock charges income (11523.90). And also, in the year 2008-2009 port & dock charges expenses and port & dock charges income have remained at the highest point of 15496.49 lakhs and 18916.94 lakhs during the entire period of study.

As per Table No. 5.3.7, the Trust's average port & dock charges ratio for the research period remained at 69.50%. It shows that the Trust spends port & dock charges expenses of Rs.69.50 to earn port & dock charges income of Rs.100, which states that the trust has earned the net port & dock charges income of Rs.30.50 during the research period.

Standard deviation of port & dock charges expenses and port & dock charges income remained at 3094.04 lakhs and at 3033.58 lakhs during the research period. It shows the dispersion from the average in cargo handling & storage charges expenses and cargo handling & storage charges income during the period of study.

Covariance of port & dock charges expenses and port & dock charges income remained at 37.72% and at 26.30% during the research period. It indicates 37.72% and 26.30% instability in port & dock charges expenses and port & dock charges income during the period of research.

Let us also check the correlation between port & dock charges expenses and port & dock charges income. For that, researcher has worked out coefficient of correlation and coefficient of determination which were 0.9573 and 0.9164 during the period of study.

Coefficient of correlation indicates that there is a high positive correlation between port & dock charges expenses and port & dock charges income. Coefficient of determination revealed that 91.64% variation in port & dock charges expenses is because of port & dock charges income and remaining 8.36% variation is because of other factors. In other words, port & dock charges income has affected 91.64% to the port & dock charges expenses and except port & dock charges income; other factors have affected 8.36% to port & dock charges expenses during the research period.

It is apparent from Graph No.5.3.7 that there are too many ups and downs in the port & dock charges ratio during the study period. The base year is 2002-03 in which the ratio is 64.94%. Compared to the base year, the ratio has increased in the year 1999-2000 by 4.42%, then it has decreased in the years 2000-2001 by 4.35% and in 2001-02 by 21.69%, then again it has increased in the years 2003-04 by 15.57%, in 2004-05 by 13.66% and in 2005-06 by 9.23% compared to the base year, then again it has shown little decline in the year 2006-07 by 0.83% compared to the base year, then it has gone upward in the years 2007-08 by 12.62% and in 2008-09 by 16.98% compared to the base year.

Graph No. 5.3.7 PORT & DOCK CHARGES RATIO

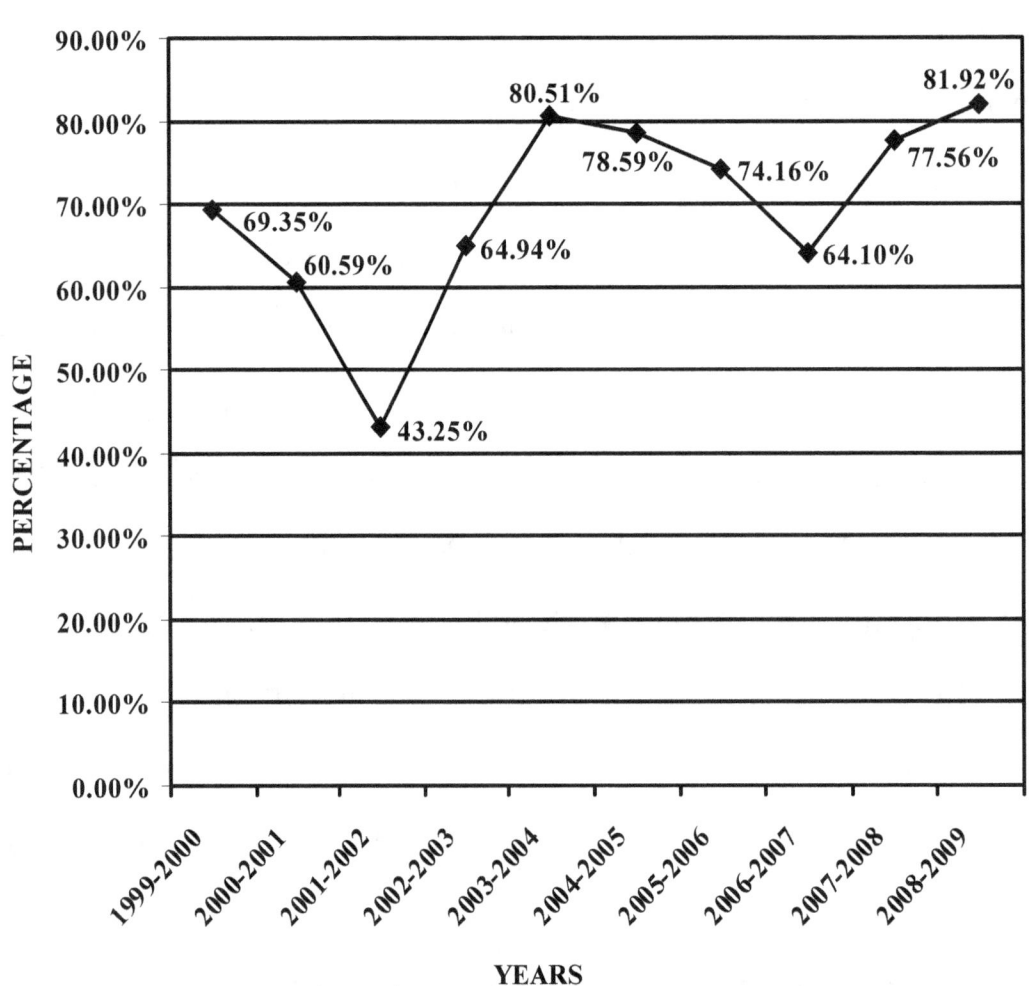

5.3.8 OPERATING EXPENSES TO INCOME RATIO:

$$= \frac{\text{Operating Expenses}}{\text{Operating Income}} \times 100$$

Table No. 5.3.8 Operating Expenses to Income Ratio

Years	Operating Expenses	Operating Income	Operating Expenses to Income Ratio
1999-2000	12642.44	22519.67	56.14%
2000-2001	11540.49	18098.42	63.77%
2001-2002	10493.36	17965.07	58.41%
2002-2003	13972.31	21197.97	65.91%
2003-2004	16557.60	21091.69	78.50%
2004-2005	17278.39	23626.59	73.13%
2005-2006	17288.15	25418.69	68.01%
2006-2007	18553.23	30041.98	61.76%
2007-2008	24796.92	34157.31	72.60%
2008-2009	32646.09	40875.89	79.87%
Minimum	10493.36	17965.07	56.14%
Maximum	32646.09	40875.89	79.87%
Average	17576.90	25499.33	67.81%
Stand. Dev.	6366.56	7027.76	
Coefficient of Variation	36.22%	27.56%	
Coefficient of Correlation = r	0.9655		
Coefficient of Determination = r^2	0.9322		

It can be seen from Table No. 5.3.8 that during the research period minimum operating expenses to income ratio is reached at the stage of 56.14% in the year 1999-2000 and maximum operating expenses to income ratio is reached at the stage of 79.87% in the year 2008-2009.

The reason for minimum operating expenses to income ratio is that in the year 1999-2000 operating expenses decreased by 28.07% and operating income decreased by 11.69% compared to average operating expenses (17576.90) and operating income (25499.33).

The reason for maximum operating expenses to income ratio is that in the year 2008-2009 operating expenses is highly increased by 85.73% whereas operating income increased by 60.30% compared to average operating expenses (17576.90) and operating income (25499.33). And also, in the year 2008-2009 operating expenses and operating income have remained at the highest point of 32646.09 lakhs and 40875.89 lakhs during the entire period of study.

As per Table No. 5.3.8, the Trust's average operating expenses to income ratio for the research period remained at 67.81%. It shows that the Trust spends operating expenses of Rs.67.81 to earn operating income of Rs.100, which states that the trust has earned the net operating income of Rs.32.19 during the research period.

Standard deviation of operating expenses and operating income remained at 6366.56 lakhs and at 7027.76 lakhs during the research period. It shows the dispersion from the average in operating expenses and operating income during the period of study.

Covariance of operating expenses and operating income remained at 36.22% and at 27.56% during the research period. It indicates 36.72% and 27.56% instability in operating expenses and operating income during the period of research.

Let us also check the correlation between operating expenses and operating income. For that, researcher has worked out coefficient of correlation and coefficient of determination which were 0.9655 and 0.9322 during the period of study.

Coefficient of correlation indicates that there is a high positive correlation between operating expenses and operating income. Coefficient of determination revealed that 93.22% variation in operating expenses is because of operating income and remaining 6.78% variation is because of other factors. In other words, operating income has affected 93.22% to the operating expenses and except operating income; other factors have affected 6.78% to operating expenses during the research period.

It is apparent from Graph No. 5.3.8 that there is fluctuating trend in the operating expenses to income ratio during the study period. The base year is 2002-03 in which the ratio is 65.91%. Compared to the base year, the ratio has decreased in the years 1999-2000 by 9.77%, in 2000-2001 by 2.15% and in 2001-02 by 7.50%, then, after the base year it has increased in the years 2003-04 by 12.59%, in 2004-05 by 7.22% and in 2005-06 by 2.10% compared to the base year, then again it has shown little decline in the year 2006-07 by 4.16% compared to the base year, then it has gone upward in the years 2007-08 by 6.68% and in 2008-09 by 13.95% compared to the base year.

Graph No. 5.3.8 OPERATING EXPENSES TO INCOME RATIO

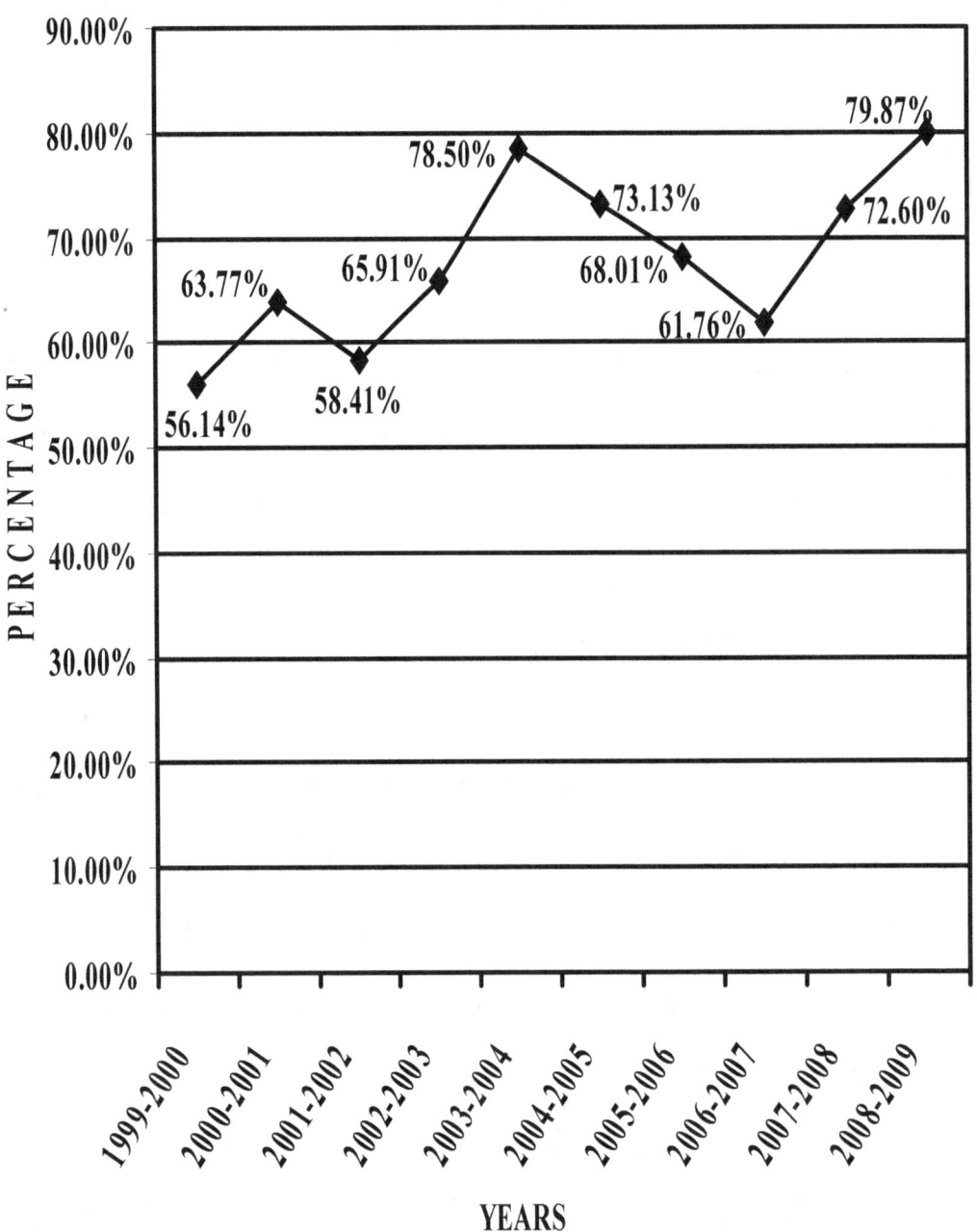

5.3.9 FINANCE & MISCELLANEOUS EXPENSES TO INCOME RATIO

$$= \frac{\text{Finance \& Miscellaneous Expenses}}{\text{Finance \& Miscellaneous Income}} \times 100$$

Table No. 5.3.9 Finance & Miscellaneous Expenses to Income Ratio

Years	Finance & Miscellaneous Expenses	Finance & Miscellaneous Income	Finance & Miscellaneous Expenses To Income Ratio
1999-2000	2850.68	14465.04	19.71%
2000-2001	4054.86	14562.18	27.85%
2001-2002	3991.33	15759.81	25.33%
2002-2003	6261.62	16242.56	38.55%
2003-2004	13162.97	17691.96	74.40%
2004-2005	1980.41	14975.07	13.22%
2005-2006	1322.63	13193.36	10.02%
2006-2007	3644.38	13473.52	27.05%
2007-2008	1071.08	16419.45	6.52%
2008-2009	4176.07	18295.39	22.83%
Minimum	1071.08	13193.36	6.52%
Maximum	13162.97	18295.39	74.40%
Average	4251.60	15507.83	26.55%
Stand. Dev.	3312.84	1604.24	
Coefficient of Variation	77.92%	10.34%	
Coefficient of Correlation = r	0.5388		
Coefficient of Determination = r^2	0.2903		

It can be seen from Table No. 5.3.9 that during the research period minimum finance & miscellaneous expenses to income ratio is reached at the stage of 6.52% in the year 2007-2008 and maximum finance & miscellaneous expenses to income ratio is reached at the stage of 74.40% in the year 2003-2004.

The reason for minimum finance & miscellaneous expenses to income ratio is that in the year 2007-2008 finance & miscellaneous expenses highly decreased by 74.81% whereas finance & miscellaneous income increased only by 5.88% compared to average operating expenses (17576.90) and operating income (25499.33). And also, in the year 2007-2008 finance & miscellaneous expenses have remained at the lowest point of 1071.08 lakhs during the entire period of study.

The reason for maximum finance & miscellaneous expenses to income ratio is that in the year 2003-2004 finance & miscellaneous expenses highly increased by 209.60% whereas finance & miscellaneous income increased only by 14.08% compared to average operating expenses (17576.90) and operating income (25499.33). And also, in the year 2003-2004 finance & miscellaneous expenses have remained at the highest point of 13162.97 lakhs during the entire research period.

As per Table No. 5.3.9, the Trust's average finance & miscellaneous expenses to income ratio for the research period remained at 26.55%. It shows that the Trust spends finance &miscellaneous expenses of Rs.26.55 to earn finance & miscellaneous income of Rs.100, which states that the trust has earned the net finance & miscellaneous income of Rs.73.45 during the research period.

Standard deviation of finance & miscellaneous expenses and finance & miscellaneous income remained at 3312.84 lakhs and at

1604.24 lakhs during the research period. It shows the dispersion from the average in finance & miscellaneous expenses and finance & miscellaneous income during the study period.

Covariance of finance & miscellaneous expenses and finance & miscellaneous income remained at 77.92% and at 10.34% during the research period. It indicates high instability of 77.92% and low instability of 10.34% in finance & miscellaneous expenses and finance & miscellaneous income during the period of research.

Let us also check the correlation between finance & miscellaneous expenses and finance & miscellaneous income. For that, researcher has worked out coefficient of correlation and coefficient of determination which were 0.5388 and 0.2903 during the period of study.

Coefficient of correlation indicates that there is a positive correlation between finance & miscellaneous expenses and finance & miscellaneous income. Coefficient of determination revealed that 53.88% variation in finance & miscellaneous expenses is because of finance & miscellaneous income and remaining 46.12% variation is because of other factors. In other words, finance & miscellaneous income has affected 53.88% to the finance & miscellaneous expenses and except finance & miscellaneous income; other factors have affected 46.12% to finance & miscellaneous expenses during the research period.

It is apparent from Graph No. 5.3.9 that there are too many fluctuations in the finance & miscellaneous expenses to income rationduring the study period. The base year is 2002-03 in which the ratio is 38.55%. Compared to the base year, the ratio has decreased in the years 1999-2000 by 18.84%, in 2000-2001 by 10.71% and in 2001-02 by 13.22%, then, it has increased in the years 2003-04 by 35.85% compared to the base year, then it has shown decreasing trend in the years 2004-05 by 25.33%, in 2005-06 by 28.53%, in 2006-07 by 11.50%, in 2007-08 by 32.03% in 2008-09 by 15.72% compared to the base year.

Graph No. 5.3.9 FINANCE& MISCELLANEOUS EXPENSES TO INCOME RATIO

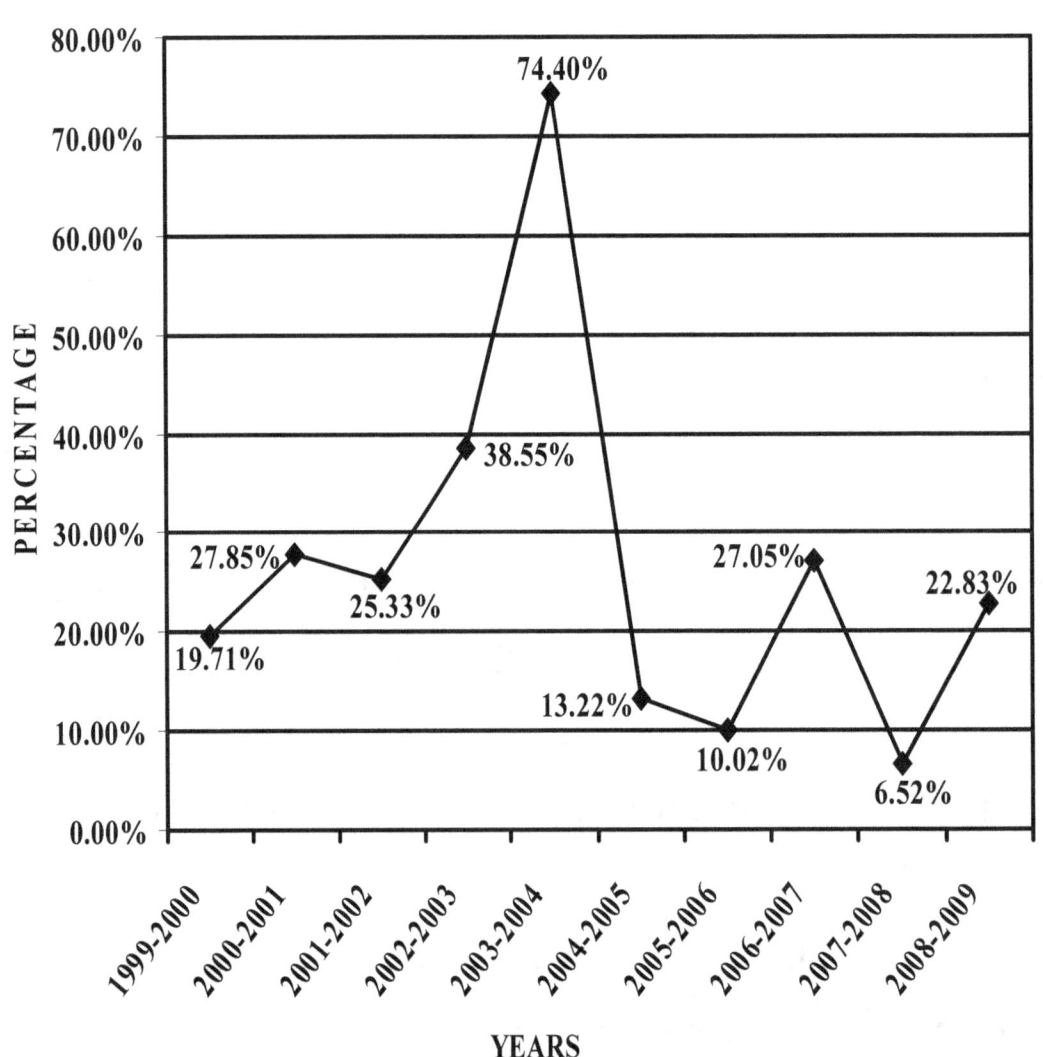

5.4 ACTIVITY RATIO:

5.4.1 FIXED ASSETS TURNOVER RATIO

$$= \frac{\text{Gross Income}}{\text{Net Fixed Assets}} \times 100$$

Table No. 5.4.1 Fixed Assets Turnover Ratio

Years	Gross Income	Net Fixed Assets	Fixed Assets Turnover Ratio (Times)
1999-2000	21142.75	36455.37	0.58:1
2000-2001	16500.44	42297.61	0.39:1
2001-2002	16539.65	47532.60	0.35:1
2002-2003	19439.51	51769.78	0.38:1
2003-2004	19568.57	55309.21	0.35:1
2004-2005	21119.14	60135.12	0.35:1
2005-2006	23569.26	68680.59	0.34:1
2006-2007	26975.69	75054.26	0.36:1
2007-2008	32451.19	77753.05	0.42:1
2008-2009	38731.21	82564.31	0.47:1
Minimum	16500.44	36455.37	0.34:1
Maximum	38731.21	82564.31	0.58:1
Average	23603.74	59755.19	0.40:1
Stand. Dev.	6816.89	14962.02	
Coefficient of Variation	28.88%	25.04%	
Coefficient of Correlation = r	0.8564		
Coefficient of Determination = r^2	0.7334		

It can be seen from Table No. 5.4.1 that during the research period minimum fixed assets turnover ratio is reached at the stage of 0.34:1 in the year 2005-2006 and maximum fixed assets turnover ratio is reached at the stage of 0.58:1 in the year 1999-2000.

The reason for minimum fixed assets turnover ratio is that in the year 2005-2006 gross income decreased by 0.15% whereas net fixed assets decreased by 14.94% compared to average gross income (23603.74) and net fixed assets (59755.19).

The reason for maximum fixed assets turnover ratio is that in the year 1999-2000 gross income decreased by 10.43% whereas net fixed assets decreased by 38.99% compared to average gross income (23603.74) and net fixed assets (59755.19). And also, in the year 19999-2000 net fixed assets have remained at the lowest point of 36455.37 lakhs during the entire period of study.

As per Table No. 5.4.1, the Trust's average fixed assets turnover ratio for the research period remained at 0.40:1. It shows that the Trust generates a gross income of Rs.40 from investment of Rs.100 in fixed assets.

Standard deviation of gross income and net fixed assets remained low at 6816.89 lakhs and at 14962.02 lakhs during the research period. It shows the less dispersion from the average in gross income and net fixed assets during the period of study.

Covariance of gross income and net fixed assets remained at 28.88% and at 25.04% during the research period. It indicates 71.12%

(100 – 28.88) and 74.96% (100 –25.04) stability in gross income and net fixed assets during the research period.

Let us also check the correlation between gross income and net fixed assets. For that, researcher has worked out coefficient of correlation and coefficient of determination which were 0.8564 and 0.7334 during the period of study.

Coefficient of correlation indicates that there is a high positive correlation between gross income and net fixed assets. Coefficient of determination revealed that 73.34% variation in gross income is because of net fixed assets and remaining 26.66% variation is because of other factors. In other words, net fixed assets have affected 73.34% to the gross income and except net fixed assets; other factors have affected 26.66% to the gross income during the research period.

It is apparent from Graph No. 5.4.1 that there is fluctuating trend in the fixed assets turnover ratio during the study period. The base year is 2002-03 in which the ratio is 0.38:1. Compared to the base year, the ratio has increased in the years 1999-2000 by 20.45% and in 2000-01 by 1.46%, then, it has decreased in the years 2001-02 by 2.75%, in 2003-04 by 2.17%, in 2004-05 by 2.43%, in 2005-06 by 3.23% and in 2006-07 by 1.61%, then, it shows recovery and it has increased in the years 2007-08 by 4.19% and in 2008-09 by 9.36% compared to the base year.

Graph No. 5.4.1 FIXED ASSETS TURNOVER RATIO

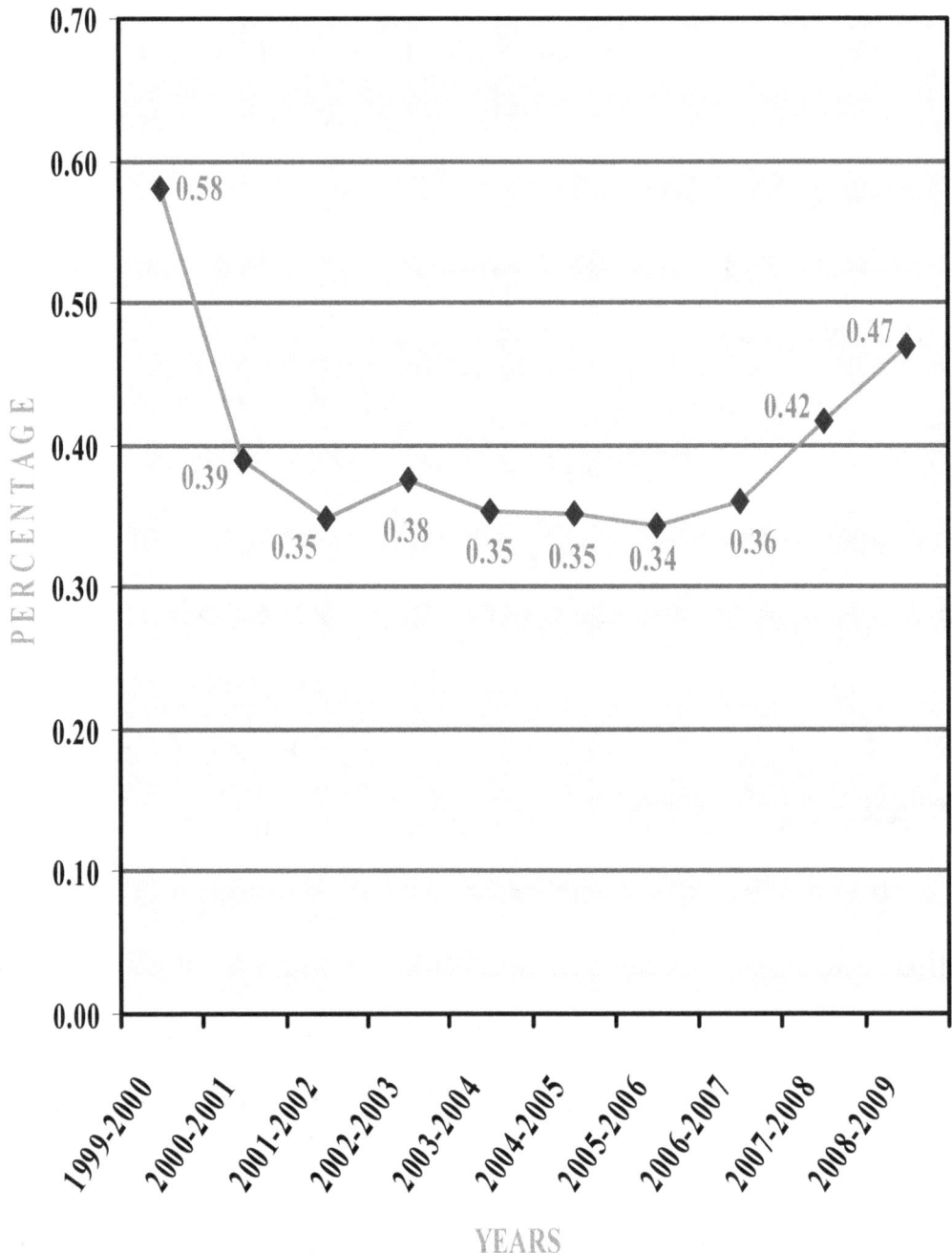

5.4.2 CURRENT ASSETS TURNOVER RATIO

$$= \frac{\text{Gross Income}}{\text{Current Assets}} \times 100$$

Table No. 5.4.2 Current Assets Turnover Ratio

Years	Gross Income	Current Assets	Current Assets Turnover Ratio (Times)
1999-2000	21142.75	101913.62	0.21:1
2000-2001	16500.44	62885.19	0.26:1
2001-2002	16539.65	61999.67	0.27:1
2002-2003	19439.51	24824.31	0.78:1
2003-2004	19568.57	16255.78	1.20:1
2004-2005	21119.14	18943.01	1.11:1
2005-2006	23569.26	18102.16	1.30:1
2006-2007	26975.69	24573.17	1.10:1
2007-2008	32451.19	36140.40	0.90:1
2008-2009	38731.21	39367.03	0.98:1
Minimum	16500.44	16255.78	0.21:1
Maximum	38731.21	101913.62	1.30:1
Average	23603.74	40500.43	0.81:1
Stand. Dev.	6816.89	26093.67	
Coefficient of Variation	28.88%	64.43%	
Coefficient of Correlation = r	-0.1990		
Coefficient of Determination = r^2	0.0396		

It can be seen from Table No. 5.4.2 that during the research period minimum current assets turnover ratio is reached at the stage of 0.21:1. in the year 1999-2000 and maximum current assets turnover ratio is reached at the stage of 1.30:1 in the year 2005-2006.

The reason for minimum current assets turnover ratio is that in the year 2005-2006 gross income decreased by 10.43% whereas current assets highly increased by 151.64% compared to average gross income (23603.74) and current assets (40500.43). And also, in the year 1999-2000 current assets have remained at the highest point of 101913.62 lakhs during the entire research period.

The reason for maximum current assets turnover ratio is that in the year 2005-2006 gross income decreased only by 0.15% whereas current assets decreased by 55.30% compared to average gross income (23603.74) and current assets (59755.19).

As per Table No. 5.4.2, the Trust's average current assets turnover ratio for the research period remained at 0.81:1. It shows that the Trust generates a gross income of Rs.81 from investment of Rs.100 in current assets.

It can be seen from Table No. 5.4.2, there are too many differences between minimum current assets turnover ratio and maximum current assets turnover ratio, because of that average current assets turnover ratio could not be revealed actual average of the Trust. Initial three years' average current assets turnover ratio is 0.25:1 and remained seven years' current assets turnover ratio is 1.05:1 of the study period. It shows the dispersion of average during the research period.

So that researcher has worked out standard deviation of gross income and current assets which were 6816.89 lakhs and 26093.67 lakhs for the study period. Standard deviation of gross income shows the dispersion of gross income of 6816.89 lakhs from the average gross income during the research period. Standard deviation of current assets shows the dispersion of current assets of 26093.67 lakhs from the average current assets during the research period.

For better understanding, researcher has also calculated Co-variance of gross income and current assets which were 28.88% and 64.43% for the study period. Co-variance of gross income shows the 28.88% instability in the gross income during the research period. Co-variance of current assets shows the 64.43% instability in the current assets during the research period.

Let us also check the correlation between gross income and current assets. For that, researcher has worked out coefficient of correlation and coefficient of determination which were -0.1990 and 0.0396 during the period of study.

Coefficient of correlation indicates that there is a low negative correlation between gross income and current assets. Coefficient of determination revealed that only 3.96% variation in gross income is because of current assets and remaining 96.04% variation is because of other factors. In other words, current assets have affected only 3.96% to the gross income and except current assets; other factors have highly affected 96.04% to the gross income during the research period.

It is apparent from Graph No. 5.4.2 that there are too many fluctuations in the current assets turnover ratio during the study period. The base year is 2002-03 in which the ratio is 0.78:1.

Compared to the base year, the ratio has decreased in the years 1999-2000 by 57.56%, in 2000-01 by 52.07% and in 2001-02 by 51.63%. After the base year, ratio has shown increasing trend and compared to the base year it has increased in the years 2003-04 by 42.07%, in 2004-05 by 33.18%, in 2005-06 by 51.89%, in 2006-07 by 31.47%, in 2007-08 by 11.48% and in 2008-09 by 20.08%.

Graph No. 5.4.2 CURRENT ASSETS TURNOVER RATIO

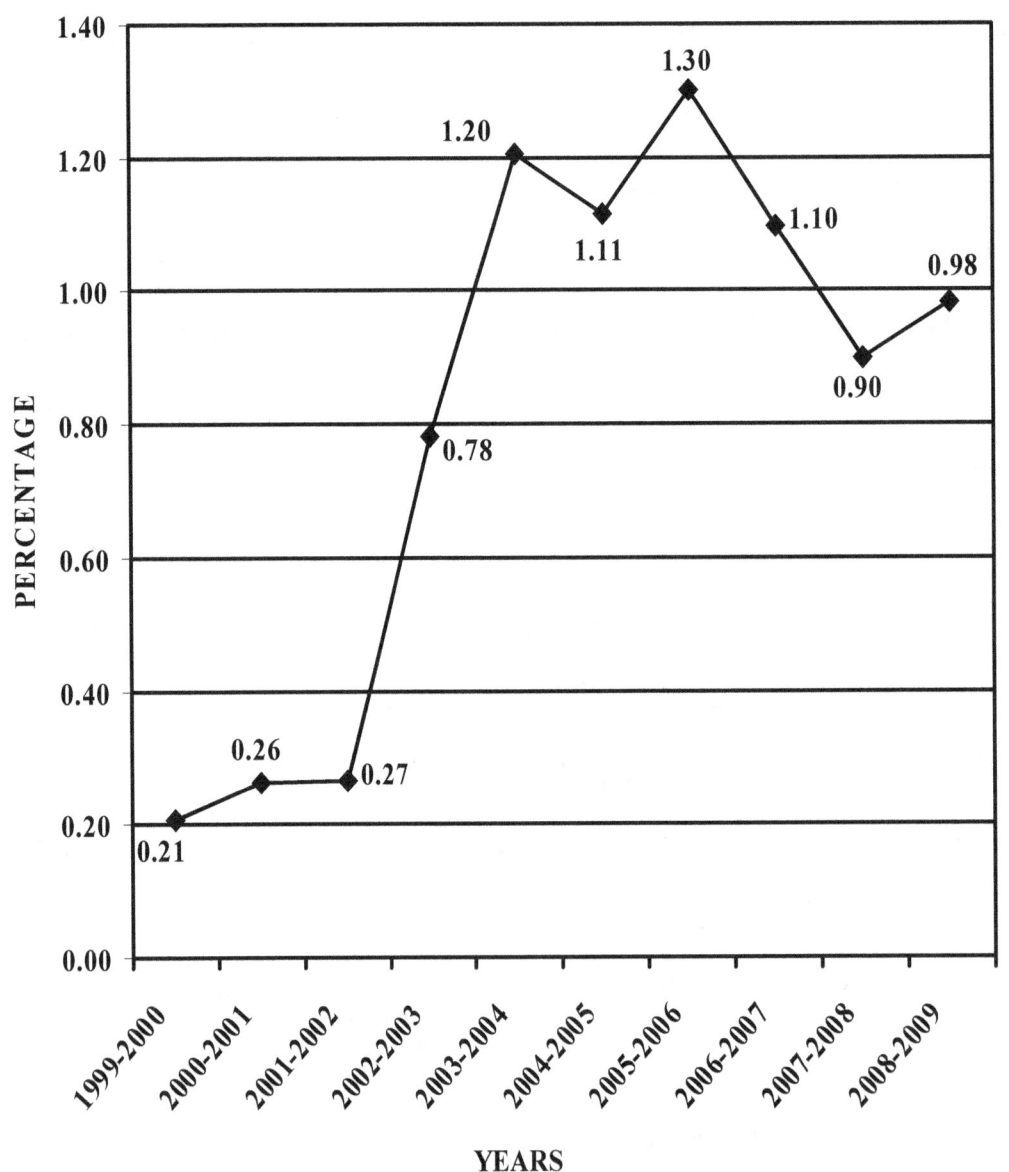

CHAPTER – 06
FINDINGS, SUGGESTIONS AND CONCLUSIONS

6.1 STATISTICAL ANALYSIS:

6.1.1 STATISTICAL ANALYSIS OF TOTAL INCOMES OF KPT:

The values of multiple R, R square and adjusted R square are one. These indicates that there exists a perfect positive correlation and linear association between Total income (dependent variable) and Cargo handling & storage charges, Port & dock charges, Estate rental, and Financial & miscellaneous income (independent variables). Because of that we can also use linear regression model.

If a level of significance of 0.05 is chosen, we can determine from table 3.2.2 that the critical value on the F distribution (with 4 and 5 degrees of freedom) is 13176.432. Where as, table value of F for (4, 5) d.f. and $\alpha = 0.05$ is 5.19. Since the calculated value of F is greater than tabulated of F, $F_C > F_t$. The difference between the calculated value of F and tabulated value of F is significant so that H_0 is rejected and H_1 is accepted.

It means that one or more β's are significant and at least one of the independent variables related to dependent variable. In simple words, Cargo handling & storage charges, Port & dock charges, Estate rental and Financial & miscellaneous income, among these four main sources of incomes at least one of the incomes is related to Total income.

6.1.2 STATISTICAL ANALYSIS OF TOTAL EXPENSES OF KPT:

The values of multiple R, R square and adjusted R square are one. These indicates that there exists a perfect positive correlation and linear association between Total expenses (dependent variable) and Cargo handling & storage charges, Port & dock facilities for shipping, Railway working, Rentable land & building, Management & general administrative expenses and Finance & miscellaneous expenses (independent variables). Because of that, we can also use linear regression model.

If a level of significance of 0.05 is chosen, we can determine from table 3.3.2 that the critical value on the F distribution (with 6 and 3 degrees of freedom) is 9967.948. Whereas, table value of F for (6, 3) d.f. and α = 0.05 is 8.94. Since the calculated value of F is greater than tabulated of F, $F_C > F_t$. The difference between the calculated value of F and tabulated value of F is significant so that H_0 is rejected and H_1 is accepted.

It means that one or more β's are significant and at least one of the independent variables related to dependent variable. In simple words, Cargo handling & storage charges, Port &dock facilities for shipping, Railway working, Rentable land & building, Management & general administrative expenses and Finance & miscellaneous expenses among these six main expenses at least one of the expense is related to Total expenses.

6.2 OBSERVATIONS OF RATIO ANALYSIS:

6.2.1 LIQUIDITY RATIO:

1) Current Ratio:

As per Table No. 5.1.1, the Trust's average current ratio for the research period remained at 476.26%. It shows that the Trust has maintained current assets of Rs.4.76 as compared to the current liabilities of Rs.1 during the study period. Trust can pay his current obligations 4.76 times during the research period. It shows strong short-term solvency and current financial liquidity of the Trust.

Whereas, C.V. of the current assets and current liabilities are 64.43% and 57.87%, which indicates instability in current assets and current liabilities during the research period. Due to this, it can be stated that if possible, Trust should concentrate more in managing stability in current assets and current liabilities.

KPT is service providing unit so there is no any closing stock and bank overdraft have been not taken during the research period so that quick ratio do not count over here.

6.2.2 CAPITAL STRUCTURE RATIO:

1) Proprietary Ratio:

As per Table No. 5.2.1, the Trust's average proprietary ratio for the research period remained at 94.18%. It shows that in comparison to investment in total of Rs.100, the Trust has maintained of Rs.94.18 as proprietary fund during the period of research.

Covariance of proprietary fund and total assets remained only at 18.29% and at 19.54% during the research period. It is indicated

81.71% (100 – 18.29) and 80.46% (100 – 19.54) stability in proprietary fund and total assets during the research period.

There is a high positive correlation between proprietary fund and total assets. Coefficient of determination revealed that 99.90% variation in proprietary fund is because of total assets and remaining only 0.10% variation is because of other factors. In other words, there is too high effect of total assets on the proprietary fund and except total assets; other factors have effected very low on the proprietary fund during the research period.

It indicates that in the total assets share of proprietary fund is huge. It shows strong lone-term solvency of the trust during the study period.

2)   Debt - Equity Ratio (As per Concept – 1):

As per Table No. 5.2.2, the Trust's average debt-equity ratio for the research period remained at 0.84%. It shows that when the investment by the Trust is of Rs.100, the investment by the outsiders is only of Rs.0.84 (i.e.84 paisa) into the total assets of Trust during the period of research.

Covariance of long-term debt and proprietary fund remained only at 4.25% and at 18.29% during the research period. It indicates 95.75% (100 – 4.25) and 81.71% (100 – 18.29) stability in long-term debt and proprietary fund during the research period.

The reasons of stability in long term-debt are as follows:

⇒ There was only one long-term debt - government loans during the research period.

⇒ Closing balance of government loans remains fixed from the year 2002-03 to 2008-09 of Rs.1611.62 lakhs.

As long term debt is fixed and there is on an average increasing trend in proprietary fund, this ratio has shown decreasing trend during the research period due to which long-term financial solvency is sustained by the trust during the research period.

3) Debt - Equity Ratio (As per Concept – 2):

As per Table No. 5.2.3, the Trust's average debt-equity ratio for the research period remained at 6.23%. It shows that when the investment by the Trust is of Rs.100, the investment by the outsiders is only of Rs.6.23 into the total assets of Trust during the period of research.

Covariance of long-term debt was indicated 50.41% instability in total debt during the study period.

The difference between this and the first concept is essentially in respect of the treatment of current liabilities. Therefore, the main reason of instability in long term-debt is current liabilities. Because of that, long-term debt-equity ratio shows fluctuating trend during the period of research.

Overall Trust has high long-term debt-equity ratio which states strong long-term financial solvency of the trust during the research period.

6.2.3 PROFITABILITY RATIO:

1) Return on Proprietors' Fund Ratio:

As per Table No. 5.3.1, the Trust's average return on proprietors' fund ratio for the research period remained at 8.67%. It shows that the Trust can earn net profit of Rs.8.67 on each investment of Rs.100 in proprietors' fund during the research period.

It is apparent from Graph No. 5.3.1 that there is fluctuating trend in this ratio during the research period. In this fluctuating trend downward trend is seen in more years than the upward trend during the research period.

So, if technically, possible this downward trend should be controlled.

2) Return on Capital Employed Ratio:

As per Table No. 5.3.2, the Trust's average return on capital-employed ratio for the research period remained at 9.51%. It shows that the Trust can earn profit before interest & tax of Rs.9.57 on each investment of Rs.100 in capital employed during the research period.

Covariance of profit before interest & tax and capital employed remained only at 21.00% and at 18.12% during the research period. It indicates 79.00% (100 – 21.00) and 81.88% (100 – 18.12) stability in profit before interest & tax and capital employed during the research period.

It shows satisfactory utilisation of capital employed by the trust due to which satisfactory rate of return is earned on capital employed during the research period.

3) Gross Profit Ratio:

As per Table No. 5.3.3, the Trust's average gross profit ratio for the research period remained at 50.20%. It shows that the Trust can earn gross profit of Rs.50.20 on the gross income of Rs.100, which states that the net gross expense is of Rs.49.80 during the research period. Covariance of gross profit and gross income remained only at 20.21% and at 28.88% during the research period. It indicates 79.79% (100 - 20.21) and 71.12% (100 - 28.88) stability in gross profit and gross income during the research period. It means that trust has sustained good profitability and sound management efficiency during the research period.

4) Operating Profit Ratio:

As per Table No. 5.3.4, the Trust's average operating profit ratio for the research period remained at 34.92%. It shows that the Trust has earned operating profit of Rs.34.92 on the gross income of Rs.100, which states that the net operating expense is of Rs.65.08 during the research period.

If we do comparison between gross profit ratio and operation profit ratio, gross profit ratio is more stable and higher than operating profit ratio. The reasons are as follows:

⇒ The C.V. of gross profit is 20.21%, whereas, C.V. of operating profit is 23.70%.

⇒ There are high positive correlation between gross income and gross profit, whereas, there are low positive correlation between operating profit and gross income and coefficient of determination comes only 20.49%.

This indicates that gross income has an effect of only 20.49% on the operating profit and except gross income; other factors have an effect of 79.51% on the operating profit during the research period.

If technically, possible Trust should decrease difference between gross profit ratio and operating profit ratio.

Above all, Trust has maintained satisfactory operating profit ratio. It shows the satisfactory operating efficiency of the Trust.

5) **Net Profit Ratio:**

As per Table No. 5.3.5, the Trust's average net profit ratio for the research period remained at 76.94%. It shows that the Trust can earn net profit of Rs.76.94 from the gross income of Rs.100 during the research period. Average net profit ratio appears higher during the research period.

There are too many variations in net profit ratio. Initial three years' average net profit ratio was 107.13% (from 1999-2000 to 2001-02), middles' four years average net profit ratio was 73.21% (from 2002-03 to 2005-06) and last three years' average net profit ratio was 51.73% (from 2006-07 to 2008-09) during research period. As per GraphNo.5.3.5 also, decreasing trend is seen in last four years. Ratio has continuously declined from 91.59% to 41.42% between the years 2004-05 to 2008-09. There is a need to stop continuous decline and make stability in net profit ratio.

Coefficient of correlation indicates that there is a very low negative correlation between net profit and gross income. Coefficient of determination revealed that only 0.0046% variation in net profit is because of gross income and remaining 99.9954% variation is because of other factors. In simple words, there is very low effect of gross income on the net profit and except gross income; other factors have highly affected the net profit during the research period.

There is very low effect of gross income on the net profit though net profit ratio came higher because of the finance & miscellaneous income and expenses. Finance & miscellaneous income have average 38.67% part in average total income where as Finance & miscellaneous expenses have average 19.65% part in average total expenses during the research period.

Above all, average net profit ratio appears higher during the research period. It means that trust has maintained satisfactory profitability and management efficiency during the research period.

6) **Cargo Handling & Storage Charges Ratio:**

The share of cargo handling and storage charges on an average is 28.85% in average total income, which states that it is one of the important areas of income for KPT during the research period.

As per Table No. 5.3.6, the Trust's average cargo handling & storage charges ratio for the research period remained at 30.89%. It shows that the Trust spends cargo handling & storage charges expenses of Rs.30.89 to earn cargo handling & storage charges income of Rs.100, which states that the trust has earned the net cargo handling, & storage charges income of Rs.69.11 during the research period.

Covariance of cargo handling & storage charges expenses and cargo handling & storage charges income indicates 50.41% and 32.24% instability in cargo handling & storage charges expenses and cargo handling & storage charges income during the period of research.

There is a high positive correlation between cargo handling & storage charges expenses and cargo handling & storage charges income. Coefficient of determination revealed that cargo handling & storage charges income has affected 90.12% to the cargo handling & storage charges expenses and except cargo handling & storage charges income; other factors have affected 9.88% to cargo handling & storage charges expenses during the research period.

No, doubt the net earning of cargo handling and storage charges is found satisfactory but as the C.V. of cargo handling and storage charges expenses remains high and correlation is also highly positive, so if possible technically, expenses should be minimized to get more fruitful results.

7)   **Port & Dock Charges Ratio:**

As per Table No. 5.3.7, the Trust's average port & dock charges ratio for the research period remained at 69.50%. It shows that the Trust spends port & dock charges of Rs.69.50 to earn port & dock charges income of Rs.100, which states that the trust has earned the net port & dock charges income of Rs.30.50 during the research period. In total expenses of the KPT the share of Port & dock charges expense is maximum during the research period.

Coefficient of determination revealed that 91.64% variation in port & dock charges expenses is because of port & dock charges income and remaining 8.36% variation is because of other factors. It means that the relation in income and expense is highly positive so if possible technically, the cost should be controlled which will result in more increase in the net port and dock charges income.

8) **Operating Expenses to Income Ratio:**

As per Table No. 5.3.8, the Trust's average operating expenses to income ratio for the research period remained at 67.81%. It shows that the Trust spends operating expenses of Rs.67.81 to earn operating income of Rs.100, which states that the trust has earned the net operating income of Rs.32.19 during the research period.

Covariance of operating expenses and operating income indicates 36.72% and 27.56% instability in operating expenses and operating income during the period of research.

There is a high positive correlation between operating expenses and operating income. Coefficient of determination revealed that operating income has affected 93.22% to the operating expenses and except operating income; other factors have affected 6.78% to operating expenses during the research period.

It means that the relation in income and expense is highly positive so if possible technically, the cost should be controlled which will result in more increase in the net operating income.

9) <u>**Finance and Miscellaneous Expense to Income Ratio:**</u>

In port normally its operating income sources are cargo handling and storage charges income and port and dock facilities income but in KPT the share in the total income is more of financial and miscellaneous income than that of stated above. Financial and miscellaneous income average share in total average income during the research period is 38.67%, while the average share of cargo handling and storage charges and port and dock facilities income are 28.85% and 27.80%.

As per Table No. 5.3.9, the Trust's average finance & miscellaneous expenses to income ratio for the research period remained at 26.55%. It shows that the Trust spends finance & miscellaneous expenses of Rs.26.55 to earn finance & miscellaneous income of Rs.100, which states that the trust has earned the net finance & miscellaneous income of Rs.73.45 during the research period.

The C.V. of financial income is 10.34% which indicates that the stability in income is by 89.66% which is one of the reasons to keep the share highest in total income.

The net earnings of KPT from finance & miscellaneous income source is strong.

There are three important pillars for any business organisation to be an excellent unit in the corporate. They are financial soundness, healthy liquidity and strong profitability. In this study it is noticed that all these three aspects are showing better result of the trust on the basis of statistical and ratio analysis. So finally the KPT can be praised by quoting as a standard unit.

6.2.4 ACTIVITY RATIO:

1)   Fixed Assets Turnover Ratio:

As per Table No. 5.4.1, the Trust's average fixed assets turnover ratio for the research period remained at 0.40:1. It shows that the Trust generates a gross income of Rs.40 from investment of Rs.100 in fixed assets.

Covariance of gross income and net fixed assets remained at 28.88% and at 25.04% during the research period. It indicates 71.12% (100 – 28.88) and 74.96% (100 –25.04) stability in gross income and net fixed assets during the research period.

There is a high positive correlation between gross income and net fixed assets. Coefficient of determination revealed that net fixed assets have affected 73.34% to the gross income and except net fixed assets; other factors have affected 26.66% to the gross income during the research period.

Finally, after examining average ratio, covariance, and coefficient of determination it can be stated that the trust has done intensive utilization of fixed assets and has maintained stability in fixed assets turnover ratio during the research period.

2)   <u>Current Assets Turnover Ratio:</u>

As per Table No. 5.4.2, the Trust's average current assets turnover ratio for the research period remained at 0.81:1. It shows that the Trust generates a gross income of Rs.81 from investment of Rs.100 in current assets.

Co-variance of current assets shows the 64.43% instability in the current assets during the research period. It is also apparent from Graph No.5.4.2 that there are too many fluctuations in the current assets turnover ratio during the study period.

There is a low negative correlation between gross income and current assets. Coefficient of determination revealed that current assets have affected only 3.96% to the gross income and except current assets; other factors have highly affected 96.04% to the gross income during the research period.

Finally, after examining average ratio, covariance, and coefficient of determination it can be stated that the trust has not done intensive utilization of current assets and shows instability in current assets turnover ratio during the research period.

6.3. RESULT OF HYPOTHESIS:

The study provide an idea about earning capacity, financial position, performance, liquidity, profitability, solvency and a comparative study within the research period of the Kandla Port Trust. The findings are how far synchronized with objective of preset study can be concluded as under:

1. The very first objective of the study was to measure the earning capacity of the firm. On the basis of this objective, the hypothesis was formed as follows,

   "Earning capacity of the firm is weak."

On the basis of statistical and ratio analysis, strong earning capacity has been found during the research period. Hence, this hypothesis is rejected.

2. The second objective of this study was to assess the financial position and performance of the firm. For this purpose the hypothesis developed was,

    "Financial position and performance of the firm are poor."

On the basis of statistical and ratio analysis, sound financial position and performance was found during the study period. Hence, this hypothesis is rejected.

3. The third objective of this study was to evaluate the liquidity, profitability and solvency of the firm. On the basis of this objective the hypothesis was formed as follows:

    "The liquidity, profitability and solvency of the firm are satisfactory."

The investigation shows very sound liquidity, profitability and solvency of the trust during the research period. Hence, this hypothesis is accepted.

4. The fourth objective of this study was to make a comparative study within the research period of the firm. On basis of this objective the hypothesis was formed as follows,

    "Comparative study within the research period of the firm remains equal."

The study shows that mixed trend was found during the research period. Hence, this hypothesis is rejected.

From the financial evaluation it is found that trust has very sound position in liquidity, profitability and financial solvency during the study period. At the same time, still trust should make efforts to sustain its existing condition and should improve its competency in the international market.

The area like financial evaluation is a broad subject for any one. For this type of study further work can be undertaken with some relevant quantitative techniques. If the comparative study between KPT and other major ports is done the KPT can be analyzed and judged from the competitive point of view. It will help to know how far better it is comparing to other major ports and in which areas its performance is weak and should be improved. More detail and keen studies should be done in this area to give fruitful results to the society.

BIBLIOGRAPHY:

➢ M.Y. Khan, P.K. Jain, Management Accounting, Fourth Edition, Tata McGraw-Hill Publishing Company Limited, New Delhi, 2007.

➢ Bharat Jhunjhunwala, Business Statistics, First Edition, S. Chand &Compny Ltd., New Delhi, 2008.

➢ C.R. Kothari, Research Methodology Methods and Techniques, Second Revised Editon, New Age Internation (P) Limited Publishers, New Delhi, 2008.

➢ R.S.N. Pillai, Bagavathi, Management Accounting Third Edition, S. Chand &Compny Ltd., New Delhi, 2008.

➢ Charles T. Horngren, Gary L. Sundem, Jhon A. Elliott, Introduction to Financial Accounting, Eighth Edition, Pearson Prentice Hall, Delhi, 2006.

➢ Asish K. Bhattacharyya, Essential of Financial Accounting, Prentice-Hall of India Private Limited, Delhi, 2007.